U.S. Department
of Transportation

**Federal Highway
Administration**

I0438695

THE FEDERAL HIGHWAY ADMINISTRATION'S

CLIMATE CHANGE &
EXTREME WEATHER
VULNERABILITY
ASSESSMENT
FRAMEWORK

DECEMBER 2012

Acknowledgements

This document was developed by Federal Highway Administration (FHWA) staff, but it draws heavily from a body of work produced for the FHWA by ICF International. It also draws from experiences and work of the North Jersey Transportation Planning Authority (NJTPA), the Metropolitan Transportation Commission (MTC), the Bay Area Conservation and Development Commission (BCDC), the California Department of Transportation District 4, the Washington State Department of Transportation (WSDOT), the Oahu Metropolitan Planning Organization (OahuMPO), the University of Virginia Center for Transportation Studies, and the many other agencies involved in the FHWA's 2010-2011 Climate Change Vulnerability and Risk Assessment Pilot Program.

Notice

Quality Assurance Statement

Table of Contents

Table of Contents

FHWA's Climate Change and Extreme Weather Vulnerability Assessment Framework

Executive Summary

The Federal Highway Administration's (FHWA's) *Climate Change and Extreme Weather Vulnerability Assessment Framework* is a guide for transportation agencies interested in assessing their vulnerability to climate change and extreme weather events. It gives an overview of key steps in conducting vulnerability assessments and uses in-practice examples to demonstrate a variety of ways to gather and process information. The framework is comprised of three key steps: defining study objectives and scope; assessing vulnerability; and incorporating results into decision making.

Defining the objectives and scope of the study at the beginning of the process is important because it creates boundaries for the analysis and can limit extraneous data collection efforts. To define study scope, agencies should first consider their overall goals and objectives. Objectives for a vulnerability assessment may include siting new assets in areas less vulnerable to climate change, educating staff regarding overall climate risks to the agency's transportation system, or informing the development of adaptation strategies. Based on these objectives, an agency can then select and characterize relevant assets and identify climate variables for study. The initial objectives and scope may be altered by the other steps in the process as new information is gathered or limitations are better understood.

Climate change and extreme weather vulnerability in the transportation context are a function of a transportation asset or system's sensitivity to climate effects, exposure to climate effects, and adaptive capacity. Tasks in the vulnerability assessment include: gathering and integrating data and information on asset location, characteristics, and climate sensitivities; gathering and obtaining information on historical weather events and projected climate; combining the asset and climate information to identify vulnerabilities; and potentially, assigning a level of risk of the climate impacts on the assets. The vulnerability assessment work is an iterative process; information gathered on assets may inform climate information needs and vice versa.

Incorporating the results of the vulnerability assessment into the agency's decision-making process ensures that the study results are used in practice. An agency may be able to use the results of the assessment in its asset management programs, hazard mitigation plans, transportation planning project selection criteria, or other programs and processes. In addition, a transportation agency might be interested in using the results of the analysis to inform the development of specific adaptation strategies for assets identified as highly vulnerable to climate change.

1   Introduction

The Federal Highway Administration (FHWA's) *Climate Change and Extreme Weather Vulnerability Assessment Framework* (hereafter, "the framework") is a guide and collection of resources for use in analyzing the impacts of climate change and extreme weather on transportation infrastructure. Its purpose is to identify key considerations, questions, and resources that can be used to design and implement a climate change vulnerability assessment. The processes, lessons learned, and resources outlined in the framework are geared toward State departments of transportation (DOTs), metropolitan planning organizations (MPOs), and other agencies involved in planning, building, or maintaining the transportation system. It includes suggestions and examples applicable to a wide range of applications, from small qualitative studies to large, detailed, data-intensive analyses. The resources included in the framework will be added to and updated over time.

The framework is informed by and draws examples from five climate change vulnerability and risk assessment pilot projects that the FHWA sponsored in 2010-2011 (hereafter, "the 2010 pilots"). The 2010 pilots were undertaken by State DOTs and MPOs to implement an earlier version of the framework, which the FHWA termed the "Vulnerability and Risk Assessment Conceptual Model." The conceptual model was meant to serve as a flexible guide for the 2010 pilots to test these basic steps and for the FHWA to obtain feedback on the suggested process. This updated framework uses the experiences of the pilots to provide some examples of the "how to" of the assessment. The 2010 pilots were:

> Climate change ***vulnerability*** in the transportation context is a function of a transportation system's exposure to climate effects, sensitivity to climate effects, and adaptive capacity.
>
> ***Exposure*** refers to whether the asset or system is located in an area experiencing direct impacts of climate change, such as temperature and precipitation changes, or indirect impacts, such as sea level rise.
>
> ***Sensitivity*** refers to how the asset or system fares when exposed to an impact.
>
> ***Adaptive capacity*** refers to the systems' ability to adjust to cope with existing climate variability or future climate impacts.

- North Jersey Transportation Planning Authority/ New Jersey Partnership - Coastal and Central New Jersey ("the New Jersey Pilot").
- Oahu Metropolitan Planning Organization - Island of Oahu ("the Oahu MPO pilot").
- Metropolitan Transportation Commission/Bay Area Conservation and Development Commission/ California Department of Transportation District 4 - San Francisco Bay ("the San Francisco Pilot").
- Virginia DOT/University of Virginia - Hampton Roads ("the Virginia Pilot").
- Washington State DOT - State of Washington ("the WSDOT pilot").

The framework also draws from the FHWA's Gulf Coast Study, Adaptation Peer Exchanges, Federal Transit Administration adaptation pilots, and other work. For more information on each of the pilots and other efforts, see Appendix A, or the FHWA's 2010 pilots website.

The vulnerability assessment framework consists of three primary components, as shown in Figure 1 and described in more detail below:

1. Defining objectives and scope.
2. Assessing vulnerability.
3. Integrating vulnerability into decision-making.

CLIMATE CHANGE AND EXTREME WEATHER VULNERABILITY ASSESSMENT FRAMEWORK

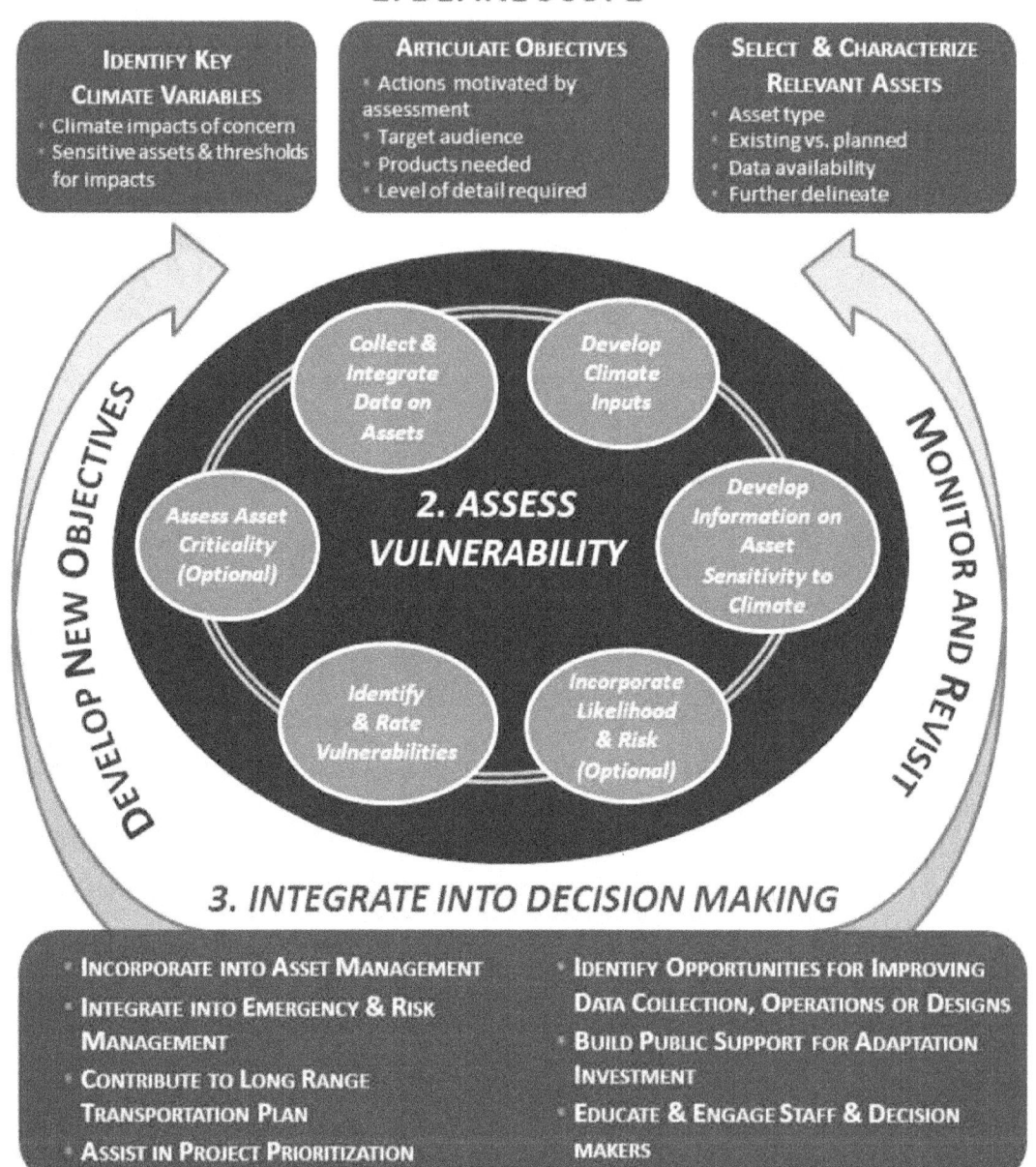

Figure 1: Climate Change and Extreme Weather Vulnerability Assessment Framework

2 Defining Objectives and Scope

This section provides suggestions and resources for articulating objectives, selecting and characterizing relevant assets, and identifying climate variables for study. Together, these steps frame the scope of the vulnerability assessment and drive the details required for the analysis. They form bounds to the study, minimizing data collection and analysis activities that would ultimately be extraneous to study objectives.

While we recommend articulating the objectives of the assessment as a first step, agencies may find it useful to simultaneously work to characterize relevant assets and identify climate variables to study.

Formulating Study Teams

Deciding who will be involved in the study has a large impact on how the study is run and the final outcomes. The members of the study team will for the most part be dictated by the study objectives. Often, a cross-disciplinary team is needed to integrate long-range planning, engineering, and asset management considerations into the vulnerability assessment effectively. For instance, each of the following disciplines may have something to offer for the study:

- Transportation planners are responsible for long-range planning of the transportation system, and regularly work with scenario planning and other tools for planning long-term investments and policies in the face of uncertain futures.
- GIS specialists can provide invaluable expertise in both analyzing and displaying transportation assets and vulnerability information.
- Asset managers may have valuable datasets and are familiar with the conditions of assets.
- State climatologists can provide information and insight into historical climate data and trends, and in some cases future projections.
- NOAA and University climate change research centers can provide projections targeted to your study area.
- Maintenance personnel often have the best on-the-ground familiarity with the ways weather events affect transportation assets today, and what it takes to maintain the system in the face of these impacts.
- Design engineers (e.g., structural, hydraulic, coastal, or other relevant disciplines) can provide input into the sensitivity of infrastructure to climate impacts and ideas/costs for adaptation solutions.
- Natural resource agency personnel can provide insight into trends in the natural environment and understanding of how projected changes might impact ecosystem services.

2.1 Articulating Objectives

It is important to identify goals and objectives early in the vulnerability assessment process as they help determine the level of detail required in the analysis and the data and products that might be needed. When developing the objectives, consider the intended outcomes and target audiences. Objectives can be based on a range of activities or goals. Some questions to consider:

What actions might be motivated by the assessment?
Who is your target audience?
What products are needed?
How will they be used?
What level of detail is required?

Example objectives include:
- Understanding the vulnerability of an agency's overall transportation system to climate change on a very general level.
- Informing the development and implementation of effective adaptation strategies.
- Integrating the vulnerability assessment into existing agency decision making processes.
- Planning for the siting or construction of new assets or services.
- Prioritizing among potential improvements or retrofits to existing assets.
- Implementing operational or design changes to mitigate climate vulnerabilities.
- Determining potential consequences from a particular type of climate impact, such as sea-level rise.
- Identifying segments or facilities at risk to climate change impacts.
- Understanding the scale and cost of climate impacts.
- Developing or augmenting data collection efforts about assets.
- Establishing or improving geo-spatial tools that can be used for transportation planning.
- Engaging stakeholders within the community or across other agencies.
- Educating transportation staff about potential risks posed by climate variability and climate change.
- Raising awareness among the public about activities to manage climate risks or efforts to bolster sustainability.

2.1.1. Examples from Practice: Articulating Objectives

Objectives deeply influence the scope and methodology of assessments. For example:

- The San Francisco pilot team's vulnerability assessment work was a part of the "Adapting to Rising Tides" (ART) project (www.adaptingtorisingtides.org), which is designed to increase the Bay Area's preparedness and resilience to sea level rise and storm events while protecting critical ecosystem and community services. The purpose of the project was to help the region's transportation and conservation planners improve vulnerability and risk assessment practices and to help formulate effective adaptation strategies. A goal of the project was to develop an approach for fostering local agency support and input on climate vulnerability and risk assessments. As such, the study team limited the study area for this initial effort a portion of one county, and limited the project scope to analyzing the impacts of sea-level rise and storm events. Many of the analysis steps involved efforts to engage stakeholders, consistent with the overall emphasis of the ART project on a collaborative planning process. The team developed detailed risk and vulnerability summaries for the most vulnerable ground transportation assets in order to inform the development of future adaptation strategies.

- The New Jersey pilot team's work represented a first step in a climate assessment for the various team members. Their project was designed to address a broad range of climate-related concerns. Their work is intended to be a platform for further assessment for other areas of New Jersey and their results will be used to engage a variety of transportation planners working at local, State, and regional levels. It included the compilation of a relatively comprehensive inventory of assets within two designated study regions, as well as the collection and analysis of a range of climate variables for the impacts analysis. The pilot team also helped to strengthen the partnerships among the agencies represented.

- The Gulf Coast Phase 2 study, which is being conducted by U.S. Department of Transportation (USDOT) in cooperation with the South Alabama Regional Planning Commission (SARPC), focuses on assessing vulnerability of Mobile, AL and developing analysis methods that can be replicated by other areas. The project also has a goal of enhancing regional decision makers' ability to understand potential impacts on specific critical components of infrastructure and to evaluate adaptation options. To this end, the study team has for the most part limited the project scope to methods and datasets that would typically be available in other study areas (with the exception of the climate information). The study team established a stakeholder group of local decision makers with which they regularly coordinate and narrowed the scope of assets for detailed study to those most important to the region.

- The Virginia Pilot study was led by researchers from the University of Virginia. The study team was interested in developing a decision support model that could be used by multiple areas, using Hampton Roads as a case study. They worked with the Hampton Roads Planning District Commission to test the model for real-world application. They have made their model available on a Web site at: http://www.virginia.edu/crmes/fhwa_climate/.

2.2   Selecting and Characterizing Relevant Assets

Transportation agencies need to decide which assets they wish to evaluate to meet the objectives of their assessment. Identifying the relevant assets for a vulnerability study and determining which characteristics of these assets to examine can help agencies narrow the scope of the vulnerability study. For example, if an agency would like to focus on a certain set of assets (e.g., owned or planned assets) it would begin the process by deciding which assets to include, assessing data availability for those assets, and understanding the timeframe and other important characteristics of managing those assets. When compiling this inventory, agencies should also gather any information that may help later to evaluate how resilient the asset is to climate stressors, and how costly damage to the asset or reductions in service could be. Example information types are provided below.

2.2.1   Asset Type

A wide range of asset types and system services could be considered in the assessment, depending on an agency's objectives. Transportation infrastructure such as roads, rails, and bridges will be a major focus for most agencies, but assets can also include support facilities, vehicles, and even ecosystem related assets for agencies interested in understanding how climate change will affect their environmental commitments or the ecosystem services on which the agency may rely. Some of the assets and systems that might be considered include:

- Bridges/tunnels
- Culverts/Storm sewers
- Road segments
- Key evacuation routes
- Rail lines, rail yards and intermodal transfer points, and passenger stations
- Transit system facilities and vehicles
- Bicycle and pedestrian facilities
- Port and airport infrastructure and access routes
- Maintenance and operations facilities
- Signals and traffic control centers
- Back-up power, communication, fueling, and other emergency operations systems
- Intelligent Transportation Systems (ITS)
- Signs and other roadside assets
- Pipelines and energy corridors
- Storm water management facilities
- Wetlands
- Floodplains
- Roadside vegetation
- Areas of potential rock fall

2.2.2   Temporal Scope

The study goals and audience may drive the temporal scope of the assets being assessed for vulnerability. If the target audience includes maintenance staff, then the study might focus on seasonal effects to existing assets. Alternatively, if the goal of the assessment is to help a metropolitan planning organization consider climate change effects in their long-term planning efforts, then it may be useful to include the future, planned assets that are in the long-range transportation plan in the universe of assets reviewed for vulnerability. In general, if the audience for the study is concerned about assets with long design lives (and planned upgrades) or assets envisioned for the future, it is important to include these assets in the analysis. For instance, the goal of the study may be to provide input to capital and rehabilitation cycles, so that new assets and upgraded assets incorporate needed adaptations.

2.2.3   Asset Data availability

Data availability can be a limiting factor on the inclusion of assets in the study scope. A variety of data is needed for climate vulnerability assessments, only some of which may be easily gleaned from standard agency databases. In some cases, necessary data may be in multiple databases or in different formats and may require significant effort to merge the information into a usable format. Typical data that might be needed for a vulnerability assessment includes:

- Age of asset
- Geographic location
- Elevation
- Current/historical performance and condition

- Level of use (traffic counts, forecasted demand)
- Replacement cost
- Repair/maintenance schedule and costs
- Structural design
- Materials used
- Design lifetime and stage of life
- LiDAR (Light Detection And Ranging) remote sensing data
- Federal Emergency Management (FEMA) maps
- Floodplain and tsunami inundation zone maps
- Vegetation and soils surveys

2.2.4   Further Delineating Assets

In most cases, time and resource constraints prevent analyzing every asset in a transportation system. An important part of scoping the study, therefore, is finding a way to delineate which assets to examine. A number of different approaches have been used:

✓ **Jurisdictional.** Agencies may choose to limit the assessment to assets that are within their control (e.g., State-owned facilities for a State DOT analysis). Though less comprehensive, this can more directly inform future actions by the agency.

✓ **Geographic.** Specific areas may be more vulnerable to some climate effects. For instance, low lying areas are more vulnerable to flooding from sea-level rise or river flooding. Agencies might focus on these areas to quickly limit the analysis to the assets most likely to be affected by climate changes.

✓ **Representative.** An agency interested in understanding the range of impacts that might affect its system could select a small number of assets that represent the different types of infrastructure and assets found in its system.

✓ **Historically poor performing or old infrastructure.** Assets that are subject to frequent flooding and debris problems or old infrastructure with little design life left may be most vulnerable to the additional stressors imposed by climate changes.

✓ **Most critical.** Another approach is to identify the most critical elements of the transportation system for analysis, using quantitative or qualitative criteria. This provides a structured way to focus on the assets that are most important for the functioning of the transportation system. For instance, this approach might be taken if the objective of the vulnerability assessment is to understand the potential impact of climate change on the evacuation routes within a region. However, sometimes defining the most "critical" assets in a system can become politicized, as stakeholders may feel that their interests are not given sufficient priority. *[See Section 2.3 for more information on conducting a criticality assessment.]*

2.2.5   Examples from Practice: Selecting and Characterizing Relevant Assets

The pilot teams chose different ways of defining the scope of the assets to include. Many of these choices were related to the objectives of the overall analysis. In addition, these choices often reflected the jurisdictional boundaries of the agencies involved in the assessment or limits of the resources available. For example:

- The WSDOT Pilot team focused on transportation infrastructure that it owned, which included roads, rails, ferry terminals, and airports. They included assets already in place and funded projects (permitted and in final design), as opposed to proposed projects in transportation plans.

- The Virginia Pilot team performed analyses along four different dimensions of transportation planning, focusing on: existing assets, projects within the existing Long Range Transportation Plan, transportation analysis zones, and transportation policies.

- The San Francisco pilot team began with a list of almost 150 assets. These were narrowed down by combining assets (for example, including local streets with bike lanes and bus routes instead of looking at all three networks separately), eliminating assets that would not experience sea level rise under any of the anticipated scenarios, and ultimately focusing on representative and unique assets in the study area. These assets were evaluated to determine their specific risk and vulnerability, as well as, the risk and vulnerability of the system the asset was from. The team cited three reasons for deciding to use a set of representative and unique assets rather than a set of identified critical assets:
  - Most assets in the small study area were arguably important.
  - Determining importance would require data and detail beyond the budget and schedule of the project, and there was not enough background information on some of the facilities to perform an assessment of criticality.
  - They did not want to pass over assets that may not be "critical" but have intrinsic value to the region (such as recreational, commute or goods movement value).

- The New Jersey Pilot team conducted a detailed analysis using the statewide travel demand model to identify the zones with the greatest travel activity, and used that as a basis for determining critical corridors and assets throughout the study area.

- The Oahu MPO Pilot team used stakeholder input in a multi-day workshop to identify the areas and types of infrastructure that were considered high priority, and develop a list of five assets to focus on in subsequent analysis. The Pilot team identified several advantages of the stakeholder workshop method of identifying assets:
  - It accomplished multiple objectives in a short timeframe.
  - It helped accomplish the task with limited financial resources. Additionally, the pilot team was able to count the attendance of many workshop participants as in-kind match for Federal funding requirements.
  - It served as a method for technology transfer within the State of Hawaii and to other Pacific island nations.

- The Gulf Coast Phase 2 Study boundaries were limited to the Mobile, AL metropolitan area, a significantly smaller study area than phase one of the study. The smaller study area allowed for a more detailed analysis. The study focused on critical assets for each of six modes: highways, transit, rail, airports, ports, and land-based pipelines.

2.2.6 Resources for Selecting and Characterizing Relevant Assets

Assessing Criticality in Transportation Planning, FHWA 2011. This memo discusses approaches for narrowing the universe of transportation assets to study in a climate change vulnerability and risk assessment by assessing their "criticality" and otherwise narrowing study scope. It identifies common challenges, and draws on examples from the FHWA Adaptation Conceptual Model Pilots and the ongoing USDOT Gulf Coast Phase 2 study.

2.3 Assessing Asset Criticality

Performing a criticality assessment is one way to narrow assets for further study. It provides a structured way to identify the most important assets that an agency might wish to examine for vulnerability to climate change. Although useful, criticality assessments can be resource and data intensive. There are several approaches available for asset prioritization, falling into two broad categories (these general approaches can also be used to prioritize assets for reasons other than criticality):

Desk Review. One approach to formulating criticality criteria is to identify a broad range of criteria that capture use and access across a range of modes and systems. Assets are ranked based on data such as average daily traffic, functional classification, goods movement, emergency management, and expert judgment. Advantages of the approach include its transparency and replicability. However, lack of data on important elements of criticality, many of which are qualitative and locally specific, or not available from the private sector, could undermine results of the desk review in the eyes of the local stakeholders and decision makers. Moreover, the results are dependent on the weight applied to the various criteria; again, this weighting may not adequately capture local concerns.

Stakeholder Input. Determining asset criticality based on input from select stakeholders and local experts is a second approach to assessing criticality. With a stakeholder input approach, the project leaders will identify a group of stakeholders in the region with expert knowledge of specific interests (e.g., commercial activity, public safety, or road maintenance). The project leaders will then elicit feedback from these stakeholders on which assets are critical. Advantages of the stakeholder approach include getting buy-in from relevant stakeholders early in the process, encouraging collaboration and communication among stakeholders and actors likely to implement any adaptation strategies, accessing information that is not readily available in publicly-available datasets, and quickly assessing criticality without a lengthy research process. However, the results of the stakeholder -driven process are highly subjective, and the outcomes are dependent on the quality of the stakeholder engagement. For example, if project leaders decide to hold a workshop or series of workshops to solicit stakeholder feedback, the quality of the workshop facilitation, composition of workshop attendees, and level of participation from key experts will be important factors in the ultimate success of the stakeholder input approach.

Often, the two approaches are combined. Typically, a desk review will identify an initial list of critical assets based on commonly available data such as average daily traffic or economic information for the region (e.g., data on imports/exports from a particular port). The project team will then use the results of the desk review to inform and structure feedback from stakeholders and local experts.

2.3.1 Examples from Practice: Assessing Criticality

- The New Jersey pilot used the desk review approach. They developed a GIS based tool to conduct a "destination-based" criticality assessment, considering jobs, population density, average annual daily traffic, and ridership data. They note that their GIS criticality assessment tool "provides agencies with a robust platform to support smart decision-making, but it is not intended to substitute for the judgment and discretion of agency officials."

- The Oahu MPO pilot used the stakeholder input approach. They held a two-day multi-disciplinary workshop to identify five critical assets for further study.

- The WSDOT pilot also used the stakeholder input approach. In workshops around the State, WSDOT employees with local knowledge rated facilities for criticality on a ten-point scale. Note that while they developed criticality ratings, the WSDOT study assessed the climate vulnerability of all assets, not just those identified as critical. *[See Figure 2]*

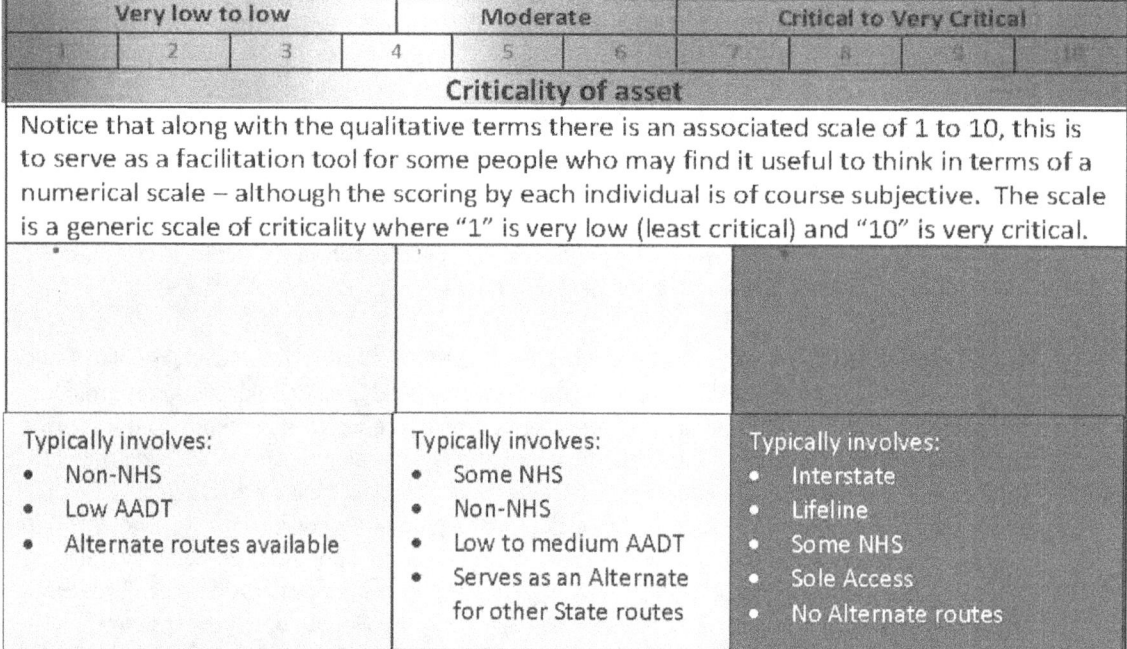

Very low to low				Moderate		Critical to Very Critical			
1	2	3	4	5	6	7	8	9	10
Criticality of asset									
Notice that along with the qualitative terms there is an associated scale of 1 to 10, this is to serve as a facilitation tool for some people who may find it useful to think in terms of a numerical scale – although the scoring by each individual is of course subjective. The scale is a generic scale of criticality where "1" is very low (least critical) and "10" is very critical.									
Typically involves: • Non-NHS • Low AADT • Alternate routes available				Typically involves: • Some NHS • Non-NHS • Low to medium AADT • Serves as an Alternate for other State routes		Typically involves: • Interstate • Lifeline • Some NHS • Sole Access • No Alternate routes			

Figure 2: WSDOT Criticality Rating Scale

- The Gulf Coast 2 project used a combined desk review and stakeholder input. A matrix of socioeconomic, operational, and health and safety characteristics of each potential asset was developed to "score" each asset for criticality. The scoring was done through a combination of quantitative measures and qualitative best judgment. A redundancy analysis was performed using the regional travel demand model to test the effect that losing particular links in the network had on congestion. The list of assets developed from this scoring system was supplemented with input from the study stakeholder group. The involvement of the stakeholder group was essential, since one of the lessons learned was that the "desk review" did not capture all the assets regarded as critical by local stakeholders. For instance, stakeholder input led to the inclusion of the Bayou La Batre port, home to a fishing and shrimping fleet with seafood processing facilities deemed important to the Mobile economy.

2.3.2 Criticality Assessment Resources

Assessing Criticality in Transportation Adaptation Planning, FHWA, 2011. This memo discusses approaches for narrowing the universe of transportation assets to study in a climate change vulnerability and risk assessment by assessing their "criticality" and otherwise narrowing study scope. It identifies common challenges, and draws on examples from the FHWA Adaptation Conceptual Model Pilots and the ongoing USDOT Gulf Coast Phase 2 study.

Assessing Infrastructure for Criticality in Mobile, AL: Final Technical Memo, FHWA, 2011. This memo summarizes the methodology and findings of Task 1 of the Gulf Coast Phase 2 study, which identified the transportation infrastructure components most critical to the Mobile region.

2.4 Identify Key Climate Variables to Study

An important first step to a vulnerability assessment is identifying which climate variables should be included in the study. Not all changes to the future climate will be significant to the local or regional transportation network, and limiting the study to the key variables of interest may allow for more in-depth projections of these variables. Section 3.3 includes more detailed information on developing climate information.

2.4.1 Key climate variables to consider

A range of future changes to the climate are of importance to transportation systems. Which ones are important to a specific transportation agency will vary by region and by study objectives. For transportation, the most important changes are often not changes to annual or seasonal averages, but to relatively short duration extreme events that can cause significant damage to transportation infrastructure or disrupt transportation operations. Examples of the kinds of climate changes included in transportation vulnerability assessments are broadly outlined below:

✓ **Temperature.** Temperature is projected to increase in almost every part of the country in the coming decades. For transportation, some impacts of interest might include increases in the number of very hot days, heat waves, changes to freeze-thaw cycles, and changes to the length of the construction season.

✓ **Extreme Precipitation Events.** Parts of the United States are projected to get wetter in the future while others will get dryer. However, many of the most significant transportation impacts will likely come from extreme precipitation events, which are projected to intensify. This poses flooding risks to roads, rails, maintenance facilities, and other assets, with below grade infrastructure such as tunnels, and poorly drained facilities being particularly vulnerable. Some areas will experience cycles of extended drought followed by extreme precipitation events which may destabilize vegetation along hillsides and increase the likelihood of rockfall.

✓ **Sea-Level and Coastal Storm Surge.** Sea-level is already rising along the U.S. coastlines, and the rate of sea-level rise is projected to accelerate over the coming century. This presents the risk of permanent or periodic inundation of coastal infrastructure as well as increased coastal erosion, rising groundwater levels and changes in salinity and it poses additional risks during storms by increasing storm surge heights as compared to today. In addition, coastal storms may intensify in the future, further increasing storm surge levels.

✓ **Permafrost Thaw.** In Alaska, much transportation infrastructure is built on permafrost foundations. Warming temperatures in the Arctic are already causing damage by thawing permafrost.

✓ **Snowmelt Hydrology.** Changes in winter snow accumulation, the timing and rate of spring snowmelt, and changes from a snow dominant to a rain dominant regime can cause an imbalance in the sediment transport characteristics of rivers, leading to flooding and channel instability problems for transportation infrastructure that is built alongside or crosses rivers.

2.4.2   Selecting climate variables to study

The climate variables selected will most likely be influenced by agencies' experiences regarding the system's performance in the past in response to the local weather, especially during extreme weather conditions such as high winds, heat waves, flooding caused by heavy precipitation or coastal storms, or drought. Examining transportation system performance during historic weather events can aid in understanding the sensitivity of the transportation system to weather extremes and aid in selection of the climate variables and thresholds to examine in the projections, providing information that can be used to gauge impacts associated with future climate conditions.

An assessment of past weather-related disruption and damage may consider:

- Weather related sources of disruption to transportation services.
- Transportation assets currently affected by weather extremes.
- Damage to roads or bridges, or supporting infrastructure (e.g., culverts).
- Thresholds at which the system begins to experience impacts (e.g., a specific high temperature or a peak flow rate that has led to damage or failure).
- Locations within the system that experience impacts.

The historical information can provide a foundation from which to identify future vulnerabilities and the climate variables/thresholds that should be addressed in the projections. For example, if heat waves pose problems for transportation systems or assets, then the model projections for temperature during the spring, summer, and fall months should be investigated closely (increases in winter temperatures are unlikely to result in "heat waves" for most locations). A specific variable to consider might be the frequency of days over 95 degrees Fahrenheit in the future, which might affect restrictions on construction or operations work crews, or perhaps information on likely exceedances of the temperature threshold applied in a particular materials specification or guidance.

While these thresholds should inform the variables for which projections are run, it is also important to be mindful of the potential of climate effects previously experienced rarely, if at all. For instance, in coastal areas it may make sense to consider projections of sea-level rise even if sea levels or tides have not been a concern in the past. [*See section 3.4 for additional discussion of climate sensitivity.*]

2.4.3   Options for Obtaining Climate Information

One consideration in determining what climate variables to look at may be the availability of future climate data for your study area, given the resources at your disposal. Information on projected changes in climate can be obtained in several different ways, including:

- Refer to existing climate information developed by others, like the Unites States Global Change Research Program (USGCRP),that is relevant at broad geographical scales, as noted above. Preliminary questions on potential impacts may be answered by referring to broader regional reports on changes in climate.

- Use climate data that has already been downscaled to your area for other studies. Some States and metropolitan areas have developed downscaled climate data for State or city climate action plans. These data can then be used for a more detailed transportation analysis.

- Work with climate modelers to develop projections tailored to your needs. This can be a resource intensive approach, but can be used to generate detailed information for your analysis. (This approach is discussed further in the Analysis section below.)

- Use information that is being used for other studies in your State or region in order to be consistent and reduce stakeholder confusion.   For example, California has established sea-level rise guidelines, as have Florida and the US Army Corps of Engineers (USACE).

Transportation agencies may want to partner with other groups that have experience developing or using climate projections. Useful sources of information and assistance include:

✓ State Climatologist – In some States, the State climatologist may be able to provide information on current climate research projects and existing projections that you could use that are relevant to your study region.

✓ University climate research centers located in your region may already be doing research on regional climate projections, and may be able to provide available data or be interested in partnering on your research effort.

✓ State and local environmental or other agencies may be able to help provide or develop necessary data. For example, local agencies may have access to LiDAR data or other data relevant to coastal mapping.

✓ Experts in the area who can offer advice or assistance in developing projections.

✓ Federal agencies such as NOAA, USGS, USACE that have data, modeling, historic weather data, and future climate predictions.

✓ The emergency response community who have been dealing with and planning for regular all hazards events; people whose knowledge and expertise of short term events can be extrapolated into long term climate change possibilities.

2.4.4 Examples from Practice: Identifying Climate Variables for Study

The differing objectives of the pilot studies resulted in a range of approaches:

- The San Francisco pilot limited its climate variables to sea level rise, storm surge and wind-driven wave effects. Storm event impacts are already being experienced with the San Francisco Bay, and future stronger and more frequent storms is likely to be the most burdensome, near-term climate change impact to the region. The study selected sea level rise scenarios for mid- and end-of-century that were within the range of values included in the *State of California Sea-Level Rise Interim Guidance Document* (October 2010). The two sea level rise scenarios were evaluated for three tide/Bay water level conditions (mean higher high water, the 100-year extreme water level, and the 100-year extreme water level with wind-driven waves) by leveraging regional modeling results from the USGS and FEMA.

- The Gulf Coast 2 study examined temperature, precipitation, sea-level rise, and storm surge variables. New, downscaled projections of temperature and precipitation for the study area were developed for the study. Several temperature and precipitation values were chosen to be projected, including a range of annual, seasonal, and extreme values *[see Table 1]*. Sea level rise scenarios were developed based on literature reviews of global sea-level rise scenarios and an assessment of historic subsidence/uplift rates specific to the area, and hurricane scenarios were developed using historic storms as a base source of data.

- The Oahu MPO pilot looked at potential sea-level rise, storm surge, wind, high intensity rainfall, drought, and temperature effects on critical assets on the island of Oahu. The study made use of climate projections from published literature and storm surge modeling from University of Hawaii research conducted for FEMA.

- The New Jersey pilot looked at sea-level rise, storm surge, extreme temperatures and temperature ranges, extreme and average precipitation, drought, and inland flooding. The pilot benefitted from assistance from their State Climatologist, and hired a consultant to develop downscaled climate projections for the study area. The pilot also analyzed future floodplain expansion using a regression model developed in a FEMA-sponsored study. Inputs to the model included current and future climate variables.

- The WSDOT pilot considered all known climate threats in the Pacific Northwest: sea level rise, precipitation change, temperature change, and fire risk. The study used climate projections funded and endorsed by an act of the Washington State Legislature for use in adaptation studies, developed by the University of Washington Climate Impacts Group.

- The Virginia pilot considered sea-level rise, storm surge, extreme temperature events, and enhanced precipitation.

Table 1:
Climate Variables Used in the Gulf Coast Phase 2 Study

Variable	Mode	Analysis
Annual, seasonal and monthly precipitation	Multi	Pavement design
Annual, seasonal, and monthly average minimum, maximum, and mean temperature	Airports	Runway design
Daily high temperature: mean, 50%, 95%, and warmest day in the year during each 30-yr period	Rail	AREMA rail design/ buildings
Seasonal and annual number of days and maximum consecutive days of high temperatures at or above 95°F, 100°F, 105°F, and 110°F	Civil/ Geotech/ Pavement	Comparing high temp days' duration to existing design standards
Mean, 5%, 25%, 50%, 75%, 95%, and largest occurrences for the average minimum air temperature over four consecutive days in winter, and the average maximum temperature over four consecutive days in summer	Bridge /Rail	Comparisons to AASHTO recommendations
Mean, 50%, 90%, 95%, and 99% occurrence of the coldest day of the year during each 30-yr period	Multi	Pavement design
Maximum 7-day average air temperature per year with the % probability of occurrence during each 30-yr period (mean, 50%, 90%, 95%, 99% occurrence)	Multi	Pavement design (asphalt)
Exceedance probability precipitation for 24-hour period with a 0.2%, 1%, 2%, 5%, 10%, 20%, and 50% exceedance precipitation events (e.g., 500-yr, 100-yr, 50-yr)	Multi	Drainage/liquid storage
24-hour exceedance probabilities based on today's 0.2%, 1%, 2%, 5%, 10%, 20%, and 50% exceedance precipitation events	Multi	Drainage
Exceedance probability precipitation across four consecutive days: 0.2%, 1%, 2%, 5%, 10%, 20%, 50%, mean; Exceedance probability of precipitation across two consecutive days: 0.2%, 1%, 2%, 5%, 10%, 20%, 50%, mean	Pipeline	Historical analysis of inundation
Largest 3-day total of precipitation each season	Multi	Change in storm events

2.4.5   Resources for Identifying Key Climate Variables

Regional Climate Change Effects: Useful Information for Transportation Agencies, FHWA 2010. This document provides basic information on projected future climate change effects over the near term, mid-century and end-of-century by U.S. region.

The Use of Climate Information in Vulnerability Assessments, FHWA 2011. This memorandum focuses on the use of climate information when performing a vulnerability assessment. The memorandum includes discussion of using historical climate information and includes information on potential data sources.

3   Assessing Vulnerability

Once the objectives and scope of the study have been defined, including a general outline of relevant infrastructure and climate variables, practitioners can begin to assess the vulnerability of their assets. The form, level of effort, and detail of the vulnerability assessment will vary based on the identified objectives, goals, and other factors. The ultimate goal of the assessment is to determine how climate change may impact the transportation assets included in the study. The findings of the assessment can then be integrated into transportation decision-making processes and used to consider and prioritize measures to address the vulnerabilities.

The assessment step in the framework will use the preliminary information and data on the relevant climate variables and assets collected during the scoping of the study. However, data collection begun as a part of project scoping will continue during the vulnerability assessment. Data collection is an iterative, on-going process and is an integral part of the assessment.

Climate change and extreme weather vulnerability in the transportation context is a function of a transportation system's sensitivity to climate effects, exposure to climate effects, and adaptive capacity. Sensitivity refers to how the asset or system fares when exposed to an impact. Related to sensitivity are asset climate thresholds-the specific climate and environmental characteristics such as temperatures, water flow, or precipitation pattern that may warrant changes to the transportation asset design or materials. Section 3.1 discusses developing information on asset sensitivity to climate.
Exposure refers to whether the asset or system is located in an area experiencing direct impacts of climate change, such as temperature and precipitation changes, or indirect impacts, such as sea-level rise. To determine exposure, information on asset location, ideally including elevation information, is combined with information on the extent of the climate impacts of concern. Section 3.2 discusses asset data collection, and Section 3.3 discusses climate inputs.

Adaptive capacity refers to the systems' ability to adjust to cope with existing climate variability or future climate impacts. Are there alternate routes? How easily might impacted assets be modified to adjust to changing climate conditions? Section 3.5 discusses adaptive capacity.

Information for vulnerability assessments can come in many forms ranging from quantitative data driven GIS or spreadsheet computations to qualitative stakeholder engagement analyses based on local knowledge of vulnerabilities. In practice, a vulnerability assessment may incorporate elements of both qualitative and quantitative analyses, and there is no one-size-fits-all approach. Spatial and temporal scale, objectives, and access to resources all may dictate different techniques.

3.1   Developing Information on Asset Sensitivity to Climate

A necessary step in a vulnerability assessment is identifying the ways in which the transportation assets you are studying are sensitive to changes in the climate or to extreme weather events—that is, what are the kinds of impacts they can experience, and at what thresholds are these impacts felt? There are a number of different approaches that have been used to identify these sensitivities.

One source for sensitivity and threshold information are the standards or guidelines developed by State DOTs or other industry organizations, such as standards for designing, constructing, and maintaining infrastructure. Design standards and guidelines can be used to isolate specific climate stressors relevant to a particular asset. The relationships provided within design standards can also be used to provide quantitative indicators of an asset's sensitivity to a particular climate stressor. Transportation infrastructure is designed according to standards and guidelines that are based on detailed sets of empirical tests, asset-specific quantitative models, and other engineering analyses. Engineers use these documents to ensure that a design meets the functional specifications of a project within accepted limits and factors of safety. Design standards and guidance consider relevant climate variables—both typical climate characteristics in which the design will operate, as well as infrequent events such as violent storms, floods, and hurricanes, whose occurrence is estimated through design return periods for each hazard.

Related to design standards are design elements or relationships. For example a narrow, steep stream may be more sensitive to increased flow than a relatively flat stream with wide floodplains. The narrow stream may react more quickly and severely with rapidly rising water surface elevations and increased velocities, whereas a flat wide floodplain may be able to distribute and store the increased flow, effectively dampening the impacts. Relationships such as structure opening area to watershed size, shape and slope may be useful as proxies for broad screens of sensitivity to increasing precipitation. Incised streams, eroding stream banks, scour holes, presence of debris and signs of head cutting or presence of vertical grade control structures can also provide warnings signs of sensitivity to increased flow and instability. The ratio of culvert span or diameter to ponding depth at a roadway sag point may also provide clues as to how much extra capacity that culvert might have available to it. All these "proxy" relationships are useful for the initial sensitivity screening of assets in that they are usually easier to detect or measure without having to perform more complicated hydraulic computations.

Another approach is to draw upon an agency's experiences with system performance in the past, especially during extreme weather conditions such as high temperature, heavy precipitation, flooding, coastal storms, or prolonged lack of precipitation. Examining transportation system performance during historic weather events can aid in understanding the sensitivity of the transportation system to weather extremes and put the projected changes into context, teasing out the types of weather events and thresholds that caused impacts to transportation facilities and operations. This information can be used to gauge impacts associated with future climate conditions.

An assessment of past weather-related disruption and damage might consider:

- Weather-related sources of disruption to transportation services.
- Transportation assets currently affected by weather extremes.
- Damage to roads or bridges, or supporting infrastructure (e.g., culverts).
- Thresholds at which the system begins to experience impacts (e.g., a specific high temperature, an amount of precipitation within a day or over several days that has led to damage or failure)
- Locations within the system that experience impacts.

Some of this information can be gleaned from existing studies; for example, if case studies exist on failures of particular bridges or roads tied to weather extremes, these can be useful to develop an understanding of the variables that caused failure. Where sufficient data are available (and in a readily accessible format), maintenance and engineering logs can be consulted to find out more specifically what types of weather events caused particular failures. This can range from the particular storm surge level that closed a bridge temporarily (for safety concerns) or that caused damage to the bridge; the levels of precipitation and stream flow at particular gages tied to culvert failure. Or, it could involve examining maintenance records, and looking for links between particular changes in the conditions of pavement and heat events.

Finally, district engineers and maintenance personnel are very often quite knowledgeable on the weaknesses or vulnerabilities of the current system. Eliciting their expert opinion on sensitivities of the current system can provide another way to determine how climate can impact the assets in the study. How often does a particular road flood, and what are the weather and environmental conditions that cause it? What temperature levels lead to enhanced pavement rutting and more rapid pavement replacement? Are there certain roads that have been flooded due to coastal storms, and if so, what kind of damage occurred as a result of particular storms? Do particular areas flood regularly at high tide with mild storms?

It is important to recognize, however, that typical historical climate conditions are unlikely to be representative of all future climate conditions. Although analysis of the past can yield useful "analogs" for certain types of weather events and the resulting impacts, the climate is changing and some future climate impacts may go beyond the range of impacts that have occurred in the recent past. Furthermore, it is unlikely that the trends of past decades will persist unchanged into the future; especially on longer timescales (greater than 30 to 40 years) simply extending past trend lines into the future may underestimate future changes. For example, for all parts of the United States, the rates of warming for the 21st century are expected to be greater than the rate of warming between 1900 and 2000. Similarly, sea-level rise rates have increased in recent decades, and they are expected to increase still more in coming decades.

3.2   Collecting Data on Assets

Often the data needed for a vulnerability analysis will be found in multiple data sources that were designed for unrelated purposes and are not easily merged together. Not all data sets are of comparable quality, or in an easily accessible format (e.g., digital, geo-spatially referenced). For instance, facility elevation data may only exist in "as-built" diagrams stored on paper. Different pieces of information on the condition of the system facilities, for instance, might be found in a bridge database, a pavement asset management system, and paper copies of culvert inspection reports. Some data needed may not be collected regularly at all. The challenges of this data integration may be a factor in determining what data to collect for the analysis.

3.2.1   Examples from Practice: Experiences with Data Collection and Integration

In inventorying State-owned transportation assets, the WSDOT quickly found that the information it wanted to use was found in multiple data sources and that the information varied widely in its level of detail and the extent of descriptive information included. The project team had to allocate additional time to convert the varied data into a format that could be used with other data in the WSDOT's GIS Workbench. Some data, such as information on repeat maintenance events that the team had hoped to use to identify current vulnerabilities, was only available in the form of individual paper maintenance reports and was not practical to use for this effort. Similarly, sea level rise (SLR) analysis proved to be very complex and difficult to determine. Without accurate elevation values for the roadway and infrastructure, it was difficult to determine whether an asset would be affected by the chosen sea level rise scenarios. Given time and resource constraints, GIS analysis was limited to proximity of an asset to the sea-level rise layers used in the database.

The New Jersey pilot gathered data from numerous sources and collected it into a geo-database for querying and analysis. Table 2 details the data included in the geo-database. The pilot team experienced some challenges with the data integration. For instance, their method for determining critical assets was largely dependent on traffic analysis zone (TAZ) information. As the two New Jersey study areas crossed the boundaries of three MPOs, with three separate travel demand models, they needed to create a unified TAZ structure for the analysis. This procedure was time consuming. Agencies with robust asset management systems may have central asset inventories to use as a strong starting point. For example, SEPTA, the transit provider for Philadelphia, had budgeted resources for asset inventorying as part of an FTA-funded climate adaptation pilot. However, because of a recent FTA-funded asset management grant, SEPTA had a robust asset inventory in place and was able to significantly reduce resources devoted to this task.

Table 2:
New Jersey Pilot Data Collection Matrix (for major assets).
Source NJTPA (2012)

Asset	GIS Data	Characteristics
Roadways	NJDOT Congestion Management System (CMS)Network[1]	NJDOT CMS data used for study area coverage and volume data. Primarily higher Functional Class highways, a few county roads and collectors included.
	NJTPA Model Network	Does not cover the entire study area. Network is simplified highway stick network. Network density is higher than CMS Network and includes lower level functional classes compared to CMS.
Bridges	NJDOT Bridge Management Data Tables	2009 BMS data used to create linear bridge location shapefiles. NJDOT's bridge locations are point features and do not include length attribute data.
	BTS NTAD	National Bridge Inventory from BTS is an additional source of bridge locations.
Tunnels	NJDOT Data Tables	Tunnels feature class created from NJDOT's data tables by linear referencing from the NJDOT highway centerline feature class.
Passenger Rail	NJ Transit	Feature classes used directly as received from NJ Transit.
	Amtrak, BTS Data	BTS 2011 has Amtrak's network as a separate shapefile for download.
Freight Rail	BTS Data	Active Freight Rail data from Oak Ridge National Laboratory Network.
	DVRPC	Data made available from DVRPC, regional in extent.
Traffic Analysis Zones	NJTPA, SJTPO, and DVRPC	A Unified TAZ structure was created by merging NJTPA, SJTPO, and DVRPC's TAZ shapefiles. NJTPA's 2010 socio-economic data was used from the three data sources.
Airports	NJDOT Data Tables, BTS	Runway lengths, airport polygons.
Wetlands	NJDEP	Wetlands files provided by NJDEP.
Evacuation Routes	NJGIN	NJDOT's Highway Safety Improvement Program Evacuation Route Shapefile.
Ports	BTS Data	
	DVRPC	Port and goods movement data provided by DVPRC.
Bus Routes		Centerline bus routes shapefile from NJ Transit.
Signals	NJ Transit	NJ Transit shapefiles.
Switches		
Track		

[1] Traffic volume data, which is one of the determinants for highway criticality is not available for all features on NJDOT's centerline network. The CMS network data has link level traffic volume information for higher level functional class highways (primarily interstates/freeways, major and minor arterials, and some urban collectors).

3.3　Developing Climate Inputs for the Vulnerability Assessment

In addition to identifying infrastructure of interest, other key pieces of information that serve as inputs to the vulnerability assessment include understanding the sensitivity (and adaptive capacity) of the infrastructure to climate/weather events and, importantly, establishing the projected future climate scenarios this infrastructure will be (or is projected to be) exposed to. Development of climate information supports both the historic look at sensitivity and the assessment of future exposure:

- Information on past climate can inform agency understanding of the kind of weather and climate effects transportation to which assets are sensitive and can inform development of thresholds of future climate effects that may affect those assets. Thresholds for analysis can be developed tied to the sensitivities identified in looking at past impacts. The thresholds could be for a specific asset or a system. For instance, there might be a mean sea-level value at a storm drain outlet that causes hydraulic grade line (HGL) to go above ground somewhere in the system given the current design storm calculations. Or there might be a sea-level rise value that causes 30 percent of current storm drain systems to violate HGL and/or permanently causes standing water on 10 percent of the road network. Another example involves precipitation. A practitioner could relate design flows to a design storm event, then establish how much higher a design storm event could be so that a specific culvert does not overtop, or 10 or 30 percent of total culverts do not overtop. For both sea-level rise and precipitation (design storm event) one can calculate a rate of approach to the intolerable level based on historical measurements.

- Information on future weather patterns and climate change effects, which translates to potential exposure faced by transportation assets, should include examination and selection of a range of future climate scenarios and the effects associated with the scenarios. Projected changes in climate may include projections of particular thresholds that are deemed to matter; thresholds can be identified through a sensitivity analysis or in design standards.

The future climate is generally expressed in the form of scenario-based projections, rather than single predictions. These reflect the various uncertainties involved in climate modeling—the amount of greenhouse gases that will be emitted (which depends on the rate and nature of economic growth, technological change, and mitigation policies), climate variability, and model uncertainty. The emission scenarios are generally based on a standard set of scenarios developed for Intergovernmental Panel on Climate Change (IPCC) assessments. Each scenario represents a future path of global societal development, with assumptions regarding population growth, economic growth, and technological change, resulting in different rates of growth in greenhouse gas emissions. In order to reduce the uncertainty and bias resulting from using just one climate model, these scenarios have been used to create outputs from more than twenty major global climate models. As a result, climate projections span a range of values, for which probabilities cannot be easily assigned. This means that in order to better assess future risks, the vulnerability assessment will need to be conducted with a range of climate inputs, rather than a single climate scenario.

3.3.1   Temperature and Precipitation

Projections of changes in temperature and precipitation can be complex. For general questions or for issues covering large areas, broad geographic region modeling of changes in temperature and precipitation may be sufficient. There are several reports[2] that provide this kind of information and use it to assess impacts on particular regions of the United States and sectors within those regions. Regional climate effects information can also help inform broad planning type questions, such as those where broad trends in temperature and seasonal precipitation are of use. For other types of questions—especially when the fate of specific transportation assets or areas of similar scale are the focus of the analysis-- it is generally preferable to use more detailed information that has been processed to reflect local features/topography and conditions. Such information and procedures for developing it are becoming more available as progress is made on downscaling and regional modeling.

3.3.1.1   Examples from Practice: Temperature and Precipitation Projections

Approaches used in the New Jersey Pilot, the WSDOT Pilot, and Gulf Coast 2:

- **Modeling.** Both the Gulf Coast 2 study and the New Jersey Pilot rely on statistical downscaling methods applied to the study area. In the Gulf Coast study, the downscaling was done based on historic temperature and precipitation information recorded at five stations in the Mobile region, while in New Jersey eight stations were used. Washington State relied primarily on information developed by the University of Washington Climate Impacts Group and other information developed for the 2009 Washington Climate Change Impacts Assessment; the Washington's Climate Impacts Group downscaled information to the greater Columbia River basin.

- **Scenarios.** The three efforts all used a range of global climate models and scenarios in developing the information over a series of time periods. The New Jersey pilot used the B1 (low emissions), A1B (moderate emissions), and A2 (high emissions) scenarios and used the results from 15 models. Models were selected based on their ability to model precipitation for New Jersey. Gulf Coast 2 relied on model runs from 10 models for the B1 and A2, and four A1FI (high emissions based on fossil fuel intensive growth) (A1FI has fewer model runs available); models were selected on their ability to replicate results for North America, for both temperature and precipitation. Variables were projected over three timeframes in Washington State and Mobile, and two timeframes in New Jersey.

- **Extreme Values.** In addition to directly-calculated variables (mean/high/low temperature and mean precipitation) the assessments also developed projections for specific thresholds or extremes that were derived from the model runs under each scenario. Examples include:

  - Number of days above 95 °, 100 °, 105 ° F.
  - Maximum 7-day air temperature.
  - Average annual return period of rainfall events exceeding 1", 2", 4" per day.
  - Daily precipitation for a range of probability of occurrences (0.2%, 1%, 2%, 5%, etc.).
  - 2-day and 4-day precipitation totals for a range of exceedance probabilities .
  - Maximum 5-day cumulative rainfall depth.
  - One percent-annual-chance flood discharge.

---

[2] See USGCRP's Global Climate Change Impacts in the United States (2009).

- **Estimating river flooding from heavy precipitation.** For inland flooding from heavy rain, the New Jersey pilot analyzed the impact of climate change on the 1-in-100 year floodplains.[3] To do this, the project team used a national regression equation that was developed through a Federal Emergency Management Agency (FEMA) study.[4] The inputs to the equation are total number of frost days annually (days below freezing), maximum number of consecutive dry days annually, and maximum 5-day rainfall during a given year (mm).[5] The project team generated these inputs specific to the study area through analysis of climate models.

  Using the statistical methods described above, the estimated future floodplains in the study areas were an average 8 percent, 40 percent, and 59 percent wider in 2050 than the current 1-in-100-year flood plain under the low, medium, and high emissions scenarios[6], respectively, and an average 17 percent, 80 percent and 178 percent wider than current floodplains in 2100. 81 miles of roadways, 1120 transit bus route miles, and 26 NJ Transit track miles lie in the projected 1-in-100 year floodplain for 2100 under the medium emissions scenario.

3.3.2 Sea-Level Rise and Storm Surge

Sea-level rise and storm surge are potentially among the most destructive impacts climate change can bring to coastal transportation infrastructure. In order to characterize exposure, most studies of sea-level rise and storm surge risk rely on spatial analysis of projected inundation. The GIS can be used to map inundated areas by analyzing areas of land that fall below increased water levels under different scenarios of sea-level rise (also called the "bathtub model"), while more sophisticated approaches account for erosion, subsidence, and natural and man-made barriers that may protect certain areas from inundation, or even model the flows of water over the landscape.

As described by NOAA (2009), inundation mapping involves the following key steps:

1. Gather elevation data and elevation surfaces for coastal land areas (includes calibrating elevation to local tidal elevations);[7]
2. Project sea-level rise and/or storm surge scenarios;
3. Use GIS to overlay the water surfaces onto the digital elevation map in order to identify inundation areas;[8]

---

[3] The 1-in-100 year floodplain, also called 100 year flood or 1% flood, is the land area flooded during a heavy rain event that has a 1% chance of occurring in any given year, or in other words, on average, once every one hundred years.

[4] Thomas et al., "Effects of Climate Change on the National Flood Insurance Program in the United States – Riverine Flooding" *Watershed Management 2010*, ASCE, 2011.

[5] These are the variables found in the FEMA study to be most highly correlated with the 1% annual chance flood discharge, in cubic feet per second.

[6] The emissions scenarios are those developed by the United Nations Intergovernmental Panel on Climate Change (IPCC). The low scenario refers to the IPCC B1 scenario, the medium to A1B, and the high to A2.

[7] Calibration often involves the choice of a vertical *datum*. As defined by NOAA (2011), "A datum is a base elevation used as a reference from which to reckon heights or depths. A tidal datum is a standard elevation defined by a certain phase of the tide. Tidal datums are used as references to measure local water levels." Example tidal datums include mean higher high water and mean high water.

[8] The sea-level rise projection must be chosen to account for the vertical accuracy of the elevation data for the land (and vice versa). An accurate map requires the root mean square error of the elevation data to be smaller than the

Projections of global, or "eustatic," sea-level rise scenarios can be found in the results from the IPCC or other globally focused studies. Projections of local sea-level rise can be made more sophisticated by accounting for a range of additional factors that influence water levels at regional and local scales, such as:

- In some locations, uplift or subsidence of the land surface can have a significant effect on the rate of relative (or local) rise of sea level. Assessing changes in land subsidence or uplift is relatively straightforward. Historic rates can be calculated and then be factored into projections; this assumes that future rates will match historic rates.
- Other factors, including changes in currents, salinity/density, and perhaps wind patterns can have an impact on sea levels. These types of changes are less well understood, though the science is evolving. For instance, on the coastline between North Carolina and Massachusetts, sea-level rise rates have been much higher than the global average for the last two decades, and the trend is expected to continue. Sea-level rise rates in the area are thought to be influenced by changes in water temperature, salinity and density in the North Atlantic.[9]
- Ongoing coastal processes, such as changes in tidal flow and sediment volume, can also have a major impact on shoreline characteristics. Barrier islands and wetlands (which may be a critical defense against storm surge) may migrate or disappear, and storms, waves, and currents will continually modify the landscape as the sea-level rises and exposes more land to wave action.

Storm surge scenarios can be developed from a number of different sources. Some of the most frequently used options include:

- Using data from NOAA tide gauges on the highest observed water level (HOWL) and combining that with sea-level rise information to project the impacts of future sea-level rise and known storm impacts. The HOWL measures the highest water level at a particular station, which is linked to a particular storm (See The Potential Impacts of Global Sea Level Rise on Transportation Infrastructure). Unfortunately, this method has its problems, as gauges sometimes do not survive storms.
- Mapping the exposure under past storms, and adding in sea-level rise (a version of the "bathtub model" approach)
- Modeling storms to include sea-level rise in the modeling. Computational models such as ADCIRC or SLOSH estimate storm surge heights for historical or hypothetical storms based on the topography for a specific locale. This approach is the most sophisticated and resource intensive approach. (The Gulf Coast 2 study and the New Jersey Pilot used this approach.)
- Leveraging ongoing or past regional modeling efforts. The San Francisco study used regional models including the TRIM2D model results from USGS and FEMA Mike modeling conducted for an ongoing bay flood study. Other localities may have regional modeling of extreme tides, storm surge, or sea-level rise.

Although a simple "bathtub" approach may indicate the relative risk among areas, it may not serve as a "prediction" for how the future landscape will appear, and thus may not capture all of the vulnerabilities

---

projected change in sea-level rise (NOAA 2009). For more in-depth discussion of land elevation data resolution and accuracy, see Chapter 2 of CCSP (2009).

[9] http://www.usgs.gov/newsroom/article.asp?ID=3256&from=rss_home

faced in a particular locale. Typically, such limitations are not critical for identifying areas at risk at broad spatial scales (e.g., regionally or nationally) or communicating these risks to the general public. However, they may be important to keep in mind when such maps are used for local land use planning. The utility and accuracy of a sea-level rise and storm surge assessments depend in part on the resolution of the underlying elevation data. One standard source of elevation data, the USGS National Elevation Dataset, supplies elevation data with a horizontal resolution of 30m and 10m and vertical resolution of around +/-2.4m. However, global projected sea-level rise of up to 2m by the end of the 21st century falls within this +/-2.4m resolution. As such, maps based on the NED will generally not provide accurate predictions of exposure of specific assets. In order to obtain more useful elevation information, local assessments will likely need to rely on digital elevation models derived from high resolution LiDAR (Light Detection and Ranging) data. These data are not available in all locations, and require additional processing to use, including adjustments to the vertical datum to ensure consistency across datasets. [10]

3.3.2.1 Examples from Practice:
Sea-Level Rise and Storm Surge Approaches and Other Considerations:

- **Elevation data** — Most of the Pilots used high resolution LiDAR data, however, the Virginia Pilot used the National Elevation Dataset (NED) to supplement the LiDAR data for areas left out. LiDAR has a much higher vertical resolution, and is better for cases where project and planning decisions will be made. LiDAR data have become increasingly available in recent years, and it is a good idea to check with city or county agencies and the NOAA Coastal Service Center's Digital Coast to see if LiDAR data are available.

- **Sea level rise scenarios** – Various studies examine a range of 0.3 to 2 meters of sea level rise by 2100. It is a good idea to work with your State or local environmental counterpart to establish sea-level rise ranges; in some cases, the State or local area may already have mandates to consider specific ranges of sea-level rise. In New Jersey, the Department of Environmental Protection (and the New Jersey Pilot) chose to look at three increments: 0.5, 1.0, 1.5 meters. The San Francisco Pilot looked at 16 inches (0.4 meters) and 55 inches (1.4 meters) of sea-level rise. The Oahu Pilot examined impacts tied to 0.75 and 1.9 meters. The Gulf Coast 2 project is looking at 0.3, 0.75, and 2.0 meters.

- **Local sea level rise adjustment** – Local sea-level rise can differ from global sea-level rise due to a number of factors mentioned above, including factors such as subsidence/uplift of the land, wind patterns, salinity and density of the water, and some of these factors are better understood than others. Some studies have tried to account for these factors. For example, the New Jersey pilot accounted for local subsidence as well as salinity and temperature. Gulf Coast 2 factors in estimates of subsidence/uplift in the Mobile region based on recent satellite measurements and gauge estimates. In the Gulf Coast 1 project, rates of subsidence were calculated at three tide gauge stations and used to represent the subsidence rates for the whole Gulf Coast region. In the Gulf Coast 2 project, which focuses on one city on the Gulf Coast, rates of subsidence/uplift were calculated for multiple areas in Mobile using changes in benchmark surveys and satellite data. The two studies serve to bookend the range of options, and levels of

---

[10] Adjustments to the vertical datum are a necessary part of mapping inundation. The land elevation data are usually referenced to a vertical datum called the North American Vertical Datum of 1988 (NAVD88). This data is not tidal, meaning that a value of 0 does not equate to any particular local tide value. Correcting this issue requires converting the elevation data from NAVD88 to a tidal datum, such as mean high tide (NOAA, 2011).

sophistication, for calculating subsidence information. (This way of looking at historic change also subsumes other factors, in addition to vertical land movement.)

- **Storm surge analysis** – Analyzing the effects of storm surge can involve examining past storms combined with projected future sea-level rise and/or changes in storms tied to climate change. Various methods may be appropriate, depending on whether the results will be used for an initial screen or used to make project-level decisions. A less resource intensive (and less precise) option involves using the GIS to map combined sea-level rise and past storm surge levels; this can be done using the NOAA tide gauge data tied to past storms (that is, the highest observed water level (HOWL)). Modeling past storms using SLOSH or, using a model like ADCIRC, with adjustments to SLR or other factors is another option. Models can also be applied to model wave heights occurring on top of storm surge. Running a model like ADCIRC is quite resource-intensive, and few MPOs or DOTs have staff familiar with this model, though a model of its sophistication may be necessary to analyze project level impacts. The New Jersey pilot used SLOSH to look at several different storm scenarios. Gulf Coast 1 used SLOSH, and Gulf Coast 2 is using ADCIRC to examine the impacts of multiple storm surge scenarios. The San Francisco pilot leveraged existing FEMA modeling to obtain surge and wave height data to create inundation maps.

- **Top-down guidance on sea level rise projections** – Several State governments and government agencies have issued requirements or recommendations on assumptions for sea level rise for use in project development. Examples include California and the U.S. Army Corps of Engineers, which is responsible for overseeing navigable waters in the United States. California issued guidance on sea level rise in 2010 that mandated that all State agencies consider a range of sea level rise scenarios for 2050 and 2100; the California Department of Transportation issued its own guidance in 2011 that includes a range of sea level rise increments over the coming decades and a process for considering whether and how to include sea level rise projections in project planning.[11] The San Francisco Pilot examined transportation vulnerability to two sea level rise scenarios, 16 inches by mid-century and 55 inches by end of century, which was consistent with the California guidance. Similarly, the U.S. Army Corps released a guidance memo in 2011 that notes that sea-level rise needs to be considered on its projects and includes information on projected ranges of sea-level rise; the document also includes a step-by-step process to help users calculate and incorporate a range of local sea-level rise estimates.[12]

- **Accounting for shoreline protections, wind, and waves** – The San Francisco pilot took shoreline assets (wetlands, levees, and similar features) into account when determining the vulnerability of coastal transportation assets. This provides more actionable information than simpler studies that only identify areas lying below a certain elevation. The pilot categorized stretches of shoreline in a GIS mapping exercise into the following five categories:

---

[11] California DOT: Guidance on Incorporating Sea Level Rise (2011).
http://www.dot.ca.gov/hq/tpp/offices/orip/Updated_Climate_Change/Documents/Sea_Level_Guidance_May2011.pdf. See also: State of California Sea-Level Rise Interim Guidance Document (2010).

[12] Sea-Level Change Considerations for Civil Works Programs (2011) EC 1165-2-212
http://planning.usace.army.mil/toolbox/library/ECs/EC11652212Nov2011.pdf

1. Engineered flood protection structures (levees, flood walls)
2. Engineered shoreline protection structures (bulkheads, revetments)
3. Non-engineered berms
4. Wetlands (natural, managed, tidal flats)
5. Natural shorelines (non-wetland)

These five categories are ordered above from those that provide the most potential protection from inundation to the transportation infrastructure behind them to those that provide the least potential for inhibiting inland inundation. The project team grouped the individual shoreline assets into larger systems of protection that protected a certain area. The team examined the sea level rise scenarios under three conditions: high tide, 100-year extreme water level from storms, and 100-year extreme water level coupled with wind waves. The team then analyzed the depth of water overtopping the asset and what percent of the length of the shoreline asset system is overtopped.

3.3.3 Resources for Developing Climate Inputs for the Vulnerability Assessment

Reports:
Regional Climate Change Effects: Useful Information for Transportation Agencies, FHWA 2010. This document provides basic information on projected future climate change effects over the near term, mid-century and end-of-century by U.S. region.

Global Climate Change Impacts in the United States, US Global Change Research Program 2009. This report summarizes the impacts of climate change on the United States, looking at different regions and economic sectors.

The Use of Climate Information in Vulnerability Assessments, FHWA 2011. This memorandum focuses on the use of climate information when performing a vulnerability assessment. The memorandum includes discussion of using historical climate information and includes information on potential data sources.

Climate Projections FAQ, U.S. Forest Service Rocky Mountain Research Station. This guidebook focuses on understanding and interpreting downscaled climate projections.

Databases:
Websites for historical weather and climate data available from the NOAA National Climatic Data Center include:

- Comprehensive U.S. climate data available at: http://www.ncdc.noaa.gov/climate-monitoring/index.php#us-icon
- US Historical Climate Network (USHCN) data: http://cdiac.ornl.gov/epubs/ndp/ushcn/ushcn.html
- Data & Products http://www.ncdc.noaa.gov/oa/ncdc.html
- Climate data online http://www.ncdc.noaa.gov/cdo-web/search
- U.S. climate maps available at: http://cdo.ncdc.noaa.gov/cgi-bin/climaps/climaps.pl

Data sources that have projections of future climate change from many different models for various emissions scenarios include:

- Statistically downscaled data from the World Climate Research Programme's Coupled Model Intercomparison Project phase 3 (CMIP3): http://gdo-dcp.ucllnl.org/downscaled_cmip_projections/dcpInterface.html

- Dynamically downscaled data from the North American Regional Climate Change Assessment Program (NARCCAP): http://www.narccap.ucar.edu/. In addition, a new project funded by USGS is developing a comprehensive web-based dataset of high-resolution (downscaled) climate change projections for the entire United States

- American Association of State Climatologists http://www.stateclimate.org/

Many university climate centers have also developed their own climate projection datasets.

3.4   Identifying and Rating Potential Vulnerabilities

There are multiple ways to combine the climate and asset information to identify potential vulnerabilities, ranging from a desk review GIS or spreadsheet analysis to a stakeholder elicitation based on local knowledge of current vulnerabilities, or a combination of both.

With the desk review approach, data on assets and projected climate are combined via a geospatial map or other analytical tool to identify potential vulnerabilities.   Projected climate change impacts are represented in a GIS format along with information on the relevant assets (such as elevation, geographic location, and existing flood protection) to determine potentially vulnerable areas.

With the stakeholder input approach, potential vulnerabilities are identified by stakeholders with intimate knowledge of study area facilities. Through workshops and/or interviews, local transportation practitioners draw from their knowledge and experience to consider how changes in climate may impact transportation facilities within their purview.

3.4.1   Examples from Practice: Identifying and Rating Vulnerabilities

- The San Francisco Pilot used a desk review approach. They considered exposure, sensitivity, and adaptive capacity of assets in their assessment of sea-level rise vulnerability, giving each asset ratings of high, medium, and low for the three criteria. They then developed an overall vulnerability rating for each asset based on the ratings of the three criteria.

- The New Jersey Pilot used the desk review approach. To identify vulnerable facilities from sea-level rise, storm surge, and inland flooding, they used GIS to determine intersections between inundated areas and transportation assets. They converted the climate scenarios' projected inundation extents from raster format into polygons and conducted an intersect analysis to determine the overlap with transportation asset lines and points. Results were illustrated in GIS maps and exported to table format as in Figure 3 and Table 3, in this case indicating roadways that would be inundated by one meter of sea level rise in the coastal study area.

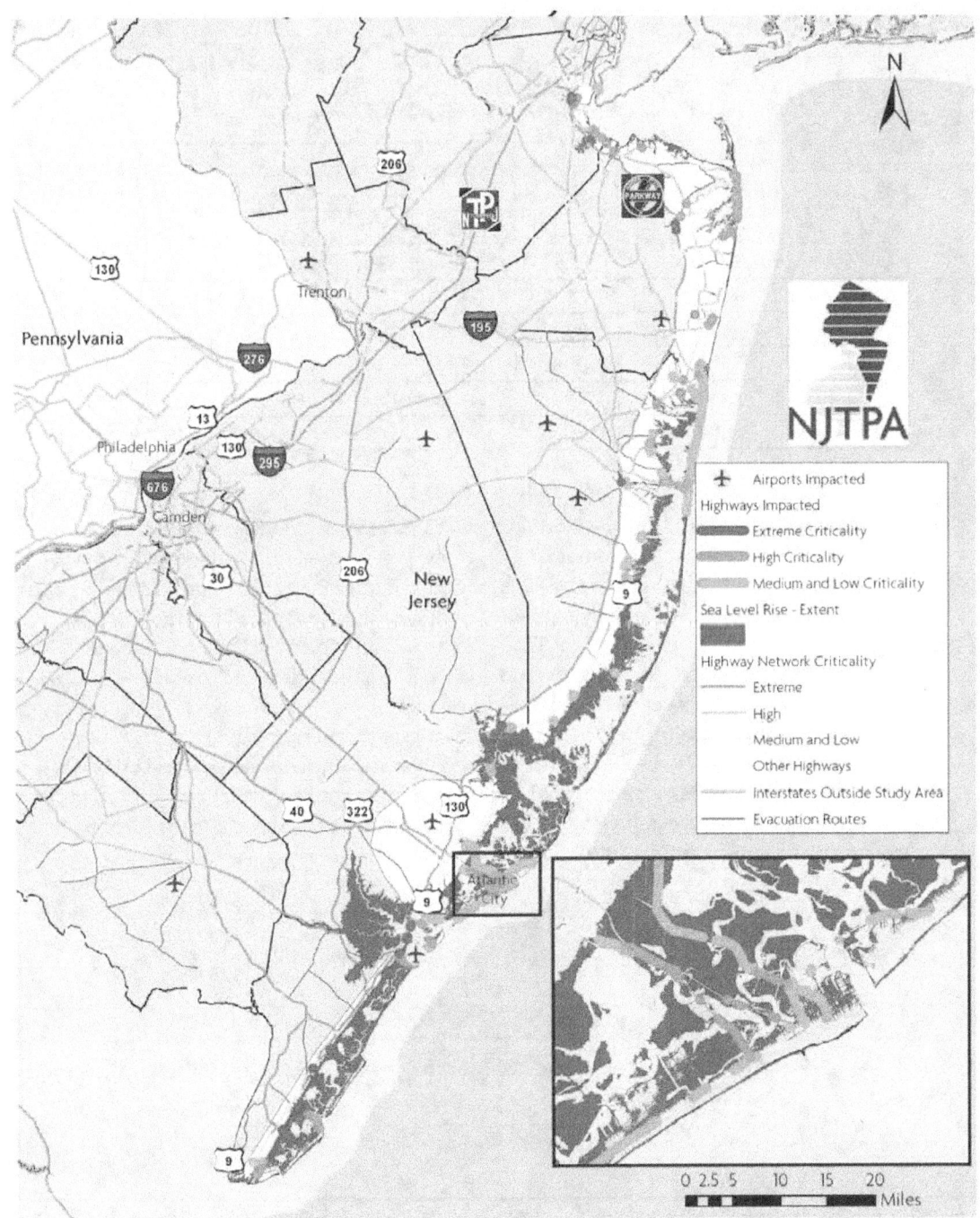

Figure 3: Roadways Inundated by 1 meter of sea level rise, coastal study area.
Source: NJTPA (2011), Cambridge Systematics.

Table 3: Roadway miles inundated by 1 meter of sea level rise, coastal study area.

Source NJTPA (2011), Cambridge Systematics

Roadway Type	Criticality Tier			Total	Increase from 2050
	Extreme	High	Med/Low		
Major Urban	0.75	11.69	28.50	**40.93**	29.62
Minor Urban	0.02	0.30	3.93	**4.26**	3.57
Major Rural	1.26	0.00	0.14	**1.40**	0.89
Minor Rural	0.00	0.00	1.83	**1.83**	1.19
Total	**2.03**	**11.99**	**34.40**	**48.42**	**35.27**
Evacuation Routes				**86.90**	71.50
NJ Transit Bus Routes				**657.88**	623.18

- The WSDOT pilot adapted a long-standing cost/risk assessment workshop model to gather stakeholder input. The study team held workshops around the State with WSDOT employees who knew each area well, such as the maintenance supervisor and their staff. Study organizers asked "What keeps you up at night?" to help identify current vulnerabilities that may be exacerbated in the future. Using projected climate information from the University of Washington and other available information, workshop participants considered likely future climate changes to sea level, temperature, precipitation, wind, and fire risks. They then assigned an impact rating to each highway segment or asset ranging from 1 to 10 using an impact rating scale scorecard (Table 4). The WSDOT's workshop participants considered asset criticality ratings as they rated the vulnerability of each facility or segment of highway. The ratings from the workshops were collected into a central database and used to create maps identifying the vulnerability level of each roadway segment or asset.

Table 4: The WSDOT Workshop Impact Rating Scale.
Source: WSDOT (2011), Adapted from Oregon Transportation Research and Education Consortium – Risk Assessment Presentation

Complete Failure

Results in **total loss or ruin of asset**. Asset *may* be available for *limited* use after at least 60 days and **would require major repair or rebuild over an extended period of time.** "Complete and/or catastrophic failure" typically involves:

- Immediate road closure.
- Travel disruptions.
- Vehicles forced to reroute to other roads.
- Reduced commerce in affected areas.
- Reduced or eliminated access to some destinations.

May sever some utilities. May damage drainage conveyance or storage systems.

Temporary Operational Failure

Results in **minor damage and/or disruption** to asset. Asset would be available with either full or limited use within 60 days. "Temporary operational failure" typically involves:

- Temporary road closure, hours to weeks.
- Reduced access to destinations served by the asset.
- Stranded vehicles.

Possible temporary utility failures.

Reduced Capacity

Results in **little or negligible impact** to asset. Asset would be available with full use within 10 days and has **immediate limited use still available.**

"Reduced capacity" typically involves:

- Less convenient travel.
- Occasional/brief lane closures, but roads remain open.
- Some vehicles may move to alternate routes.

3.5   Considering Adaptive Capacity

Adaptive capacity refers to the ability of a system to adjust to climate change (including climate variability and extremes) to moderate potential damages, to take advantage of opportunities, or to cope with the consequences.

One way in which a transportation system can have greater adaptive capacity is if it has redundant routes or modes. For instance, if a particular roadway segment is impassable due to flooding, the availability of parallel routes or alternative modes can continue to enable travel between destinations. The New Jersey pilot considered this aspect of adaptive capacity during its criticality screen. The pilot ranked assets as more highly critical if there were no alternative routes available.

Another relevant criterion is how easily and quickly service can be restored to a segment or asset following a climate-related disruption. The Gulf Coast 2 Study, for instance, is using two measurements to evaluate how quickly service could be restored to a given segment: replacement costs and time duration of disruptions. Replacement costs can provide a rough proxy for the ease in which assets could be repaired or replaced; resources are more easily mobilized for lower cost repairs, and replacement costs indicate overall complexity, size, and expense of the asset itself. Length of time for the disruption to clear (for instance, for debris to be cleared from a rail line following a storm) is an indicator of how well the system can deal with the climate impact. The availability of staffing and resources for preventive measures can also increase adaptive capacity. For instance, SEPTA, the public transportation provider for Philadelphia, provides the example of deploying maintenance crews prior to an expected storm to trim trees along rail lines in order to minimize potential for wind-blown debris from trees to block the tracks.

Key considerations for evaluating adaptive capacity include[13]:

- Is the system already able to accommodate changes in climate?
- Are there barriers to a system's ability to accommodate changes in climate?
- Is the system already stressed in ways that will limit the ability to accommodate changes in climate?
- Is the rate of projected climate change likely to be faster than the adaptability of the system?
- Are there efforts already underway to address impacts of climate change related to the system?

Ultimately, the vulnerability assessment will aid transportation decision-makers in prioritizing actions and determining how to improve the adaptive capacity of the system.

3.6   Incorporating Likelihood and Risk

In addition to determining whether an asset may be impacted by climate change, it can also be important to understand just how vulnerable the assets are. Information on risk and the timeframe of the risk are useful for determining whether climate change should be considered in project

---

[13] Snover, A.K., L. Whitely Binder, J. Lopez, E. Willmott, J. Kay, D. Howell and J. Simmonds. 2007. *Preparing for Climate Change: A Guidebook for Local, Regional and State Governments.* In association with and published by ICLEI - Local Governments for Sustainability, Oakland, CA.

development, prioritizing actions, and weighing adaptation options. However, assigning risk associated with climate change vulnerability is imprecise. It is not possible to apply a certain likelihood to a climate scenario. And further, climate models do not all agree. This section provides a brief overview of assessing climate risk to transportation assets, discusses some of the challenges to assigning a specific risk, and offers examples of some ways transportation agencies have incorporated likelihood and risk into their vulnerability assessments.

3.6.1 Assessing Risk

A risk assessment integrates the severity or consequence of an impact with the probability or likelihood that an asset will experience a particular impact. To determine consequence, transportation agencies may wish to consider the level of use of an asset, the degree of redundancy in the system, or the value of an asset (in terms of cost of replacement, economic loss, environmental impacts, cultural value, or loss of life). The consequence of projected impacts may have been a component of the vulnerability assessment discussed in Section 3.4.

Determining the probability of occurrence, or likelihood, of future climate impacts, can be problematic. As mentioned above, it is not possible to apply a particular likelihood to a climate scenario, and climate models do not all agree. With the absence of information on the likelihood of specific climate impacts, climate impact studies will often use separate risk matrices for a range of possibility with a "low emissions" scenario and a "high emissions" scenario, or a range of emissions scenarios, as discussed in Section 3.3. These studies will also use several climate models, often averaging results of those that most accurately model past regional climate, and characterizing impacts that occur under all the models "highly likely." The resultant impact projections will be split into high- to low-likelihood groupings, with the caveat that the climate may be more or less sensitive than we think. Depending on objectives and study scope, the study team may want to choose projections from one scenario or a range of scenarios. To the extent that information is available, impacts will be split into high- to low-likelihood groupings.

In general, there is much more certainty regarding the direction of change than there is regarding the magnitude of change, or the length of time it will take to reach a change. For this reason, an agency may want to consider impacts that are fairly certain to happen at some point this century, even if there is some uncertainty regarding whether the impacts will occur in 2050 or 2080. With information on consequence and likelihood, agencies can categorize assets into groups:

- Assets that have a low likelihood of being impacted by a future climate condition and a low consequence of being impacted by that condition.

- Assets that have a low likelihood of being impacted by a future climate condition and a high consequence of being impacted by that condition.

- Assets that have a high likelihood of being impacted by a future climate condition and a low consequence of being impacted by that condition.

- Assets that have a high likelihood of being impacted by a future climate condition and a high consequence of being impacted by that condition.

The integrated risk is often represented by a two-dimensional matrix that classifies risks into three categories (low, moderate, high) based on the combined effects of their likelihood and consequence. *An example matrix risk rating matrix used by the San Francisco Pilot is provided in Figure 4.*

		Consequence				
		1	2	3	4	5
Likelihood	1	2	3	4	5	6
	2	3	4	5	6	7
	3	4	5	6	7	8
	4	5	6	7	8	9
	5	6	7	8	9	10
Risk	Low		Moderate		High	

Unacceptable, major disruption likely; priority management attention required.

Moderate Risk (Orange)

Some disruption; additional management attention may be needed.

Low Risk (Green)

Minimum impact; minimum oversight needed to ensure risk remains low.

Figure 4: Risk Rating Matrix.
Source: Adapting to Rising Tides: Transportation Vulnerability and Risk Assessment Pilot Project, November 2011

3.6.2 Examples from Practice: Assessing Risk

- The San Francisco pilot assessed risk of sea-level rise to two to three representative assets per asset type identified as most vulnerable. The project team limited their study scope to "likely" sea-level rise scenarios in both mid-century and end of century, thus they considered likelihood of impact to be the same for all assets in the small study area. The study team acknowledged that the while the projections used for mid-century (16 inches) and end of century (55 inches) were not definitively tied to a specific date, the Bay will experience the amount of sea level rise evaluated at some point in the future. They developed a consequence rating for each asset included in the risk assessment by averaging ratings of six criteria. They combined likelihood and consequence ratings to calculate an overall risk rating for each asset.

- The Oahu MPO pilot used three day-long group work sessions of an interdisciplinary project team to assess integrated risk to the five priority assets in their study. At the work sessions, the team discussed likelihood, magnitude, and consequence to society of future climate change impacts to each asset. Facility operators and other subject matter experts provided past experience of the facilities to natural disasters and emergencies. Table 5 summarizes some of the results of the integrated risk assessments, in this case the risk of sea-level rise to Honolulu International Airport.

Table 5:
Sea-Level Rise Risk Assessment for Honolulu International Airport, Oahu MPO (2011).

Risk Level in Year 2050	TheBus 811 Middle Street	Low Vulnerability, Low Structural Impact
	HDOT Highways Division Oahu District Baseyard 727 Kakoi Street	Low-Moderate Vulnerability, Low Structural Impact
	Honolulu International Airport and Access	Low Vulnerability, Low Structural Impact
Risk Level in Year 2100	TheBus 811 Middle Street	Low-Moderate Vulnerability, Low-Moderate Structural Impact
	HDOT Highways Division Oahu District Baseyard 727 Kakoi Street	High Vulnerability, High Structural Impact
	Honolulu International Airport and Access	Low-Moderate Vulnerability, Low Structural Impact

- Rather than conducting a risk assessment *per se*, the New Jersey pilot developed a range of scenarios designed to capture the potential range of possibilities. The scenarios were not assigned specific likelihoods. The team used a total of three climate scenarios: low, medium, and high emissions (the B1, A1B, and A2 scenarios) for both 2050 and 2100. They applied the lowest emissions scenario to the least aggressive of 15 climate models that were deemed to best replicate the local climate, the medium emissions scenario to the median climate model, and the high emissions scenario to the most aggressive climate model, thereby creating a range of projections. Similarly, for sea-level rise they selected low, medium, and high scenarios for 2050 and 2100 in consultation with the New Jersey Department of Environmental Protection. The study team recommended that NJ jurisdictions use the range of scenarios developed for the study to examine their assets in more detail. They recommend using the high emissions/most aggressive model scenario to analyze impacts to the most critical infrastructure, and the low emissions/least aggressive scenario to analyze impacts to the least critical infrastructure. However, to narrow the scope of their pilot study, the project team performed an analysis of all assets in the study area based on the medium scenario.

3.6.3 Resource for Assessing Risk

Literature Review: *Climate Change Vulnerability Assessment, Risk Assessment, and Adaptation Approaches*, FHWA, July 2009. This document details how vulnerability, risk, and adaptation assessments have been or could be used to integrate climate change impacts into transportation decisions and ultimately increase the adaptive capacity of the highway system.

4 Integrating Vulnerability into Decision Making

Once transportation vulnerabilities are identified, a logical next step is to consider how to address them. Integrating results of the vulnerability assessment into decision making is important to ensure that study results are used in practice. While the information developed from the vulnerability assessment should be used to satisfy the study objectives, the results may also be useful in ways not initially anticipated. This section includes strategies to effectively incorporate vulnerability assessment findings into practice.

While we include several in practice examples in this section, the FHWA's initial round of vulnerability assessment pilot projects was for the most part limited to the vulnerability assessment itself. The FHWA will sponsor a second round of pilots with a goal of helping further the State of the practice in applying vulnerability assessment results into decision making.

4.1   Identifying, Analyzing and Prioritizing Adaptation Options

Transportation agencies may choose to focus their efforts on those assets identified in the vulnerability assessment as having high likelihood of climate impact and high consequence. For these assets, detailed analysis of the costs and benefits of adaptation strategies could be conducted. Strategies might include engineering new assets to withstand environmental conditions anticipated in the future (e.g., construction materials better suited to higher heat days), retrofitting existing assets (e.g., adding barriers to prevent water incursion into tunnels), more intensive maintenance schedules (e.g., more frequent cleaning of drains), systems planning (e.g., siting new facilities outside of expanded flood plains), and improved operations plans for weather emergencies. Adaptation strategies should be evaluated based on cost savings from avoided impacts as well as implementation costs. Strategies should also be evaluated based on their feasibility, efficacy, ability to withstand a range of climate hazards, and co-benefits.

Not many agencies have conducted these analyses to date. As such, the FHWA anticipates making this section of the framework more robust based on experience with the second round of pilots.

4.2   Incorporating Vulnerability Assessment Results into Transportation Programs and Processes

Incorporating vulnerability assessment results into existing and updated processes can be an effective mechanism to implement lessons learned quickly and comprehensively. Use of the vulnerability assessment results in this way can be seen as improving existing analysis and practice, rather than as a separate and distinct activity. Considering climate change as one of many risks to be considered in transportation decision-making rather than as a separate issue lowers barriers to adaptation. Agencies may be able to incorporate climate change vulnerability assessment results into:

- o   asset management;
- o   emergency and risk management;
- o   hazard mitigation plans;
- o   transportation planning project selection criteria; or
- o   environmental review.

The asset management process is a natural fit for incorporating climate change and extreme weather vulnerability information. In many cases, existing infrastructure may not be up to handling climate change and extreme weather events. Consideration of resilience, replacement, and restoration of assets can be integrated into asset management programs. Work on a vulnerability assessment can serve as a launch point to begin looking at a State's asset management system from the standpoint of climate resilience.

State DOTs and MPOs have a strong interest in integrating climate change adaptation, hazard mitigation, and transportation planning into a holistic planning process. In many communities, hazard mitigation occurs separately from local planning processes, including transportation planning. This practice can sometimes result in land use and transportation planning that inadvertently encourages development in hazardous areas.

4.2.1   Examples from Practice: Incorporating Results into Transportation Programs and Processes

- The WSDOT incorporated results of their vulnerability assessment into their Guidance for Project-Level Greenhouse Gas and Climate Evaluations (March, 2012). The guidance calls for project teams to review the vulnerability assessment results as a first step to answering the question "How will my project be affected by climate change?" The WSDOT maps developed as part of the assessment summarize the assessment results, and can be used by project teams to identify potential vulnerabilities in their project area. The WSDOT has published several Environmental Impact Statements and NEPA Environmental Assessments containing information about the relationship of the proposed project to a changing climate.

- The Virginia Pilot developed a tool for incorporating vulnerability and risk assessment results into the transportation planning process. The decision support tool helps to prioritize projects in a transportation plan based on how they would address various issues, including climate change vulnerability.

- The Boston MPO incorporated climate vulnerability information into their transportation planning process. To help identify areas where transportation infrastructure may be vulnerable to natural hazards and to inform the security evaluation of proposed transportation projects, the MPO undertook a hazard mapping project. They created an interactive Web tool that maps the transportation network, natural flood zones, bridge condition, emergency routes, and emergency support facilities. The tool links to the MPO's database of Transportation Improvement Program (TIP) projects and can be used to determine whether proposed projects are located in areas exposed to flooding, storm surge, or sea-level rise. During project evaluations, the MPO asks, "Will the project enable the facility to function in extreme weather conditions?" and "Does it improve a facility that provides redundancy in a vulnerable area?" www.bostonmpo.org/hazards

- The Los Angeles County Metropolitan Transportation Authority (LACMTA) recently added climate adaptation considerations into its construction contracts. Under the environmental provisions section of the contract, LACMTA specifies that the contractor must consider projected climate impacts in the design and construction of the project and refers contractors to the 2011 Federal Transit Administration (FTA) research report, "Flooded Bus Barns and Buckled Rails: Public Transportation and Climate Change Adaptation," for more information. LACMTA is currently undertaking an FTA-funded project to integrate climate change information and adaptation into the agency's robust environmental management system (EMS).

- The Metropolitan Atlanta Rapid Transit Authority (MARTA), the public transportation provider for Atlanta, is incorporating climate impacts into its asset management system, including the software system used for analyzing data on asset condition and prioritizing capital investments. The public transportation providers for Philadelphia and Chicago (SEPTA and CTA) are similarly marrying climate adaptation efforts with federally-funded asset management efforts.

- Chittenden County MPO in Vermont is currently working with a Department of Housing and Urban Development (HUD) grant to integrate climate change adaptation, hazard mitigation, and transportation into a single planning document.

- The Maryland State Highway Administration (MDSHA) uses its asset management system as a climate adaptation tool. The agency collects data related to climate change and extreme weather vulnerability in its Transportation Asset Management Program (TAMP) to better analyze priority assets. These data include age, elevation, materials used, design lifetime and stage of life, FEMA flood maps, current and historical performance and conditions, vegetation, soil type, average daily traffic, bridge scour criticality, and length and width of bridges.[1] The MDSHA has mapped and identified roads, bridges, and culverts vulnerable to sea level rise. In addition, using 2011 road closure coordinates from CHART (Coordinated Highways Action Response Team), the MDSHA plotted a GIS map labeled by category for the type of road closure such as high water, debris, winter precipitation, or other type of incident. The analysis proved useful for the agency's vulnerability assessment as well as during emergency operations. For instance, during Hurricane Sandy in October 2012, the State emergency management agency used the 2011 road closure data layer in a geographic data mapping system called Osprey to combine many other data layers and identify potential hazards. The Osprey system used historical data on traffic and road closures collected by SHA to help improve storm response.[2]

- The San Francisco pilot selected two vulnerable assets to test a methodology for analyzing adaptation options. Using the information in the risk profiles developed by the project, the team held a work session to evaluate strategies based on equity, economy, ecology, and governance. The team notes that this was an initial, qualitative assessment that will need further investigation to determine the real cost-effectiveness, applicability, and viability of proposed adaptation measures.

  One of the assets evaluated was the San Francisco-Oakland Bay Bridge touchdown and toll plaza on the Oakland side. The asset is protected by a combination of engineered shoreline protection and wetlands. Even so, the shoreline protection would be overtopped under the mid and late century sea level rise plus 100-year storm scenarios. This would inundate the bridge touchdown and toll plaza as well as other transportation assets in the area (Interstate 80, West Grand Avenue, Mandela Parkway, Burma Road, 7th Street Highway and Railroad Pumps, and Union Pacific Martinez subdivision).

---

[1] Slater, Gregory I., "Climate Change Adaptation: Maryland State Highway Administration," Presentation to U.S. Department of Transportation, March 30, 2011.

[2] Eugene Mulero and Julia Pyper, "As states scramble to adapt, DOT pledges $13M in first of many likely cash infusions," *Greenwire*, October 21, 2012.

For asset-specific adaptation measures for midcentury, the team considered improved drainage, retrofit, and raised road surface. Improved drainage around the freeway and toll plaza would mean that when inundation occurs, there might be only partial closure of the roadway and, after a storm/high tide event, water would drain off the road surface quickly enough to minimize disruption. Retrofitting to better withstand temporary inundation would include placing wiring and electronics for the toll plaza above the flood elevation and waterproofing buildings and toll booths. Raising the road surface in areas identified as particularly vulnerable could be done as part of regularly scheduled maintenance. For end-of-century, more expensive measures may warrant consideration such as elevating the entire freeway above the end-of-century 100-year storm level. This might also provide benefits to the region because the raised road could serve as a levee protecting West Oakland.

The team also considered regional adaptation measures for midcentury—creating a berm, supporting wetland growth, and constructing a floodwall. For end-of-century the team considered constructing levees, raising a floodwall built at midcentury, and building new wetlands (It is unlikely that wetlands will be able to keep pace with sea level rise at the end of the century).

4.2.2 Resources for Incorporating Results into Transportation Programs and Processes

FHWA Adaptation Peer Exchanges Final Report, FHWA, August 2012. This report synthesizes key themes and lessons from a series of three FHWA-sponsored peer exchanges on climate change adaptation, including examples of effective implementation practices presented by the MPO and State DOT participants.

Flooded Bus Barns and Buckled Rails: Public Transportation and Climate Change Adaptation, FTA, 2011. This comprehensive FTA report on climate change adaptation for public transit includes a chapter on implementation of climate change adaptation strategies at transportation agencies. There is also a case study on Transport for London's experience with asset management.

Eligibility of Activities to Adapt To Climate Change and Extreme Weather Events Under the Federal-Aid and Federal Lands Highway Program, FHWA, 2012. This memo clarifies that Federal-aid and Federal Lands highway funding may be used for climate change adaptation work. The memo notes that creating a more resilient transportation system is a priority for the FHWA and provides some examples of eligible uses of Federal-aid and Federal Lands highway funds to consider the potential impacts of climate change and extreme weather events and apply adaptation strategies.

4.3 Stakeholder Engagement and Communication

It is difficult to overstate the importance of public stakeholder engagement in vulnerability assessment and adaptation planning. If the target audience does not buy into the vulnerability assessment, it may not support the resulting adaptation actions. The appropriate method of engaging stakeholders will vary according to the agency, context, and objectives. It is very important to plan for a specific target audience, and agencies often engage different groups of stakeholders in stages.

Successful engagement of internal staff requires listening and incorporating their feedback and perspective. If these staff members are engaged and feel that they can take ownership over the strategy, they may be more willing to provide valuable leadership and insight.

Communicating the need for climate change adaptation is challenging for several reasons. First, people often assume that "climate change" issues refer exclusively to mitigation. Organizations and government agencies often house climate change adaptation efforts within traditional environmental programs, even though adaptation impacts multiple programs, including asset management, risk mitigation, operations, and planning. Second, the term climate change has become politicized, inhibiting public agency communication and action in those jurisdictions where political forces do not wish to address the issue. Lastly, it is difficult to communicate the range of uncertainty associated with climate projections. For example, agencies are often concerned about releasing detailed inundation maps, which might alarm and alienate coastal property owners because it is difficult to describe the specific assumptions and uncertainties associated with these maps. Almost any adaptation assessment effort will show increased vulnerability to flooding for coastal properties, but acknowledging potential additional flooding vulnerability decreases the economic value of the property.

4.3.1 Strategies for Effective Communication

The 2010 pilots and participants in the FHWA sponsored peer exchanges have identified several strategies for effectively communicating climate change vulnerability:

- In order to avoid confusing the issue of climate change adaptation with the politics of climate change mitigation, some agencies use the terms "extreme events," "event management," "all-hazard management," and "resilience" as effective terms for communicating impacts and adaptation issues.
- Another strategy for communicating the need for adaptation is to expand conceptions of sustainability and asset preservation to include resilience. Agencies can emphasize that climate change adaptation is simple, good business practice that should be integrated throughout the agency.
- Frame adaptation as better planning and responsible risk management.
- Frame adaptation as saving money. Stress that preventing impacts is almost always cheaper than cleaning up and rebuilding after an extreme weather event.
- Use past events, such as a memorable flood or heat wave, to help communicate the meaning of climate projections.
- Highlight possible solutions to climate impacts. Frame the issue as one of rising to the challenge.
- Use graphics.
- Tailor the message to your audience.
- Talk in the here and now. Explain how the climate is already changing in the geographic area the audience is concerned with and the impact on assets and services that the audience values. (Many individuals are not aware that climate change impacts are already occurring.)

5   Next Steps

Creating a more resilient transportation system is a priority for the FHWA and is consistent with a recent U.S. DOT policy statement on climate change adaptation.[14] Analyzing and incorporating potential future climate change impacts to transportation systems is a relatively new and evolving area of practice. One of the FHWA's goals is to ensure that State DOTs, MPOs, and local partners have the capacity to address this relatively new area in their transportation plans and programs. A way that the FHWA is working toward this is by developing and sharing information on tools and methodologies, such as those highlighted in this document, that State DOTs and MPOs can use to assess climate change vulnerability and risk, and to prioritize actions.

The FHWA plans to sponsor a new round of pilot projects in late 2012 through early 2014 to help fill in gaps in this framework and to assist MPOs and State DOTs to advance climate change adaptation activities more quickly. The FHWA anticipates that the selected pilots will fall into two distinct groups:

1) A continuation of vulnerability assessments similar to the first set of pilots only focused on concerns specific to the interior portions of the country.
2) Advancement beyond the initial vulnerability assessment stage to development and implementation of adaptation options.

Information on the new round of pilots, along with other FHWA research activities will be available on the FHWA's Climate Change Adaptation website.

---

[14] US DOT, Policy Statement on Climate Change Adaptation, June 2011. The Policy statement noted DOT's intention to integrate consideration of adaptation into its planning, operations, policies, and programs, and also described some of the guiding principles. See: http://www.dot.gov/docs/climatepolicystatement.pdf

Appendix A:
Vulnerability Assessment Summaries

The WSDOT Study

The Washington State Department of Transportation (WSDOT) assessed the infrastructure it owns, including roads, rail, ferry facilities, and airports. The WSDOT held workshops around the State, presenting information on climate projections and asking maintenance engineers and other employees with intimate familiarity with the assets, "What keeps you up at night?" to help identify current vulnerabilities that may be exacerbated in the future.

Washington State Department of Transportation, *Climate Impacts Vulnerability Assessment*, November 2011.

The New Jersey Study

The New Jersey project was led by the North Jersey Transportation Planning Authority and was supported by an interagency partnership, including the three New Jersey MPOs, the New Jersey Department of Transportation, New Jersey Transit, the New Jersey Department of Environmental Protection, and the New Jersey State Climatologist. The pilot closely followed the three steps of the Conceptual Risk Assessment Model in its analysis of the New Jersey Turnpike/I-95 corridor and the New Jersey Coast.

New Jersey Transportation Planning Authority, *Climate Change Vulnerability and Risk Assessment of New Jersey's Transportation Infrastructure*, April 2012.

The OahuMPO Study

The Oahu Metropolitan Planning Organization (MPO) used an interagency, multidisciplinary 2-day workshop to facilitate a climate change dialog and identify five key vulnerable assets for further study. The five assets were then assessed in more detail by transportation experts in three full-day work sessions.

Oahu Metropolitan Planning Organization, *Transportation Asset Climate Change Risk Assessment*, November 2011.

The Virginia Study

The University of Virginia developed a priority setting tool to assess how consideration of climate change and other factors may affect project prioritization in a transportation plan. The State used the Hampton Roads region as a case study.

University of Virginia and Virginia Department of Transportation, *Assessing Vulnerability and Risk of Climate Change Effects on Transportation Infrastructure, Hampton Roads, VA Pilot*, November 2011.

The San Francisco Study

The Metropolitan Transportation Commission, in partnership with the San Francisco Bay Conservation and Development Commission, the California Department of Transportation District 4, and others, led a study of a portion of the Bay, stretching from the San Francisco-Oakland Bay Bridge to the San Mateo Bridge (Alameda County). This study was focused on sea level rise. The project team developed profiles of risk to sea level rise for a list of representative and unique assets within the study area, including exposure, sensitivity, and adaptive capacity.

Metropolitan Transportation Commission, Caltrans, Bay Conservation and Development
Commission, *Adapting to Rising Tides: Transportation Vulnerability and Risk Assessment Pilot
Project: Briefing Book,* November 2011.

The Gulf Coast Study

To better understand potential climate change impacts on transportation infrastructure and
identify adaptation strategies, the US DOT is conducting a comprehensive, multi-phase study of
climate change impacts in the Central Gulf Coast region. This region is home to a complex
multimodal network of transportation infrastructure and several large population centers, and it
plays a critical national economic role in the import and export of oil and gas, agricultural products,
and other goods. The study is sponsored by the US DOT's Center for Climate Change and
Environmental Forecasting in partnership with the USGS and is managed by the FHWA.

Gulf Coast Phase 1

Phase 1 (completed in 2008) examined the impacts of climate change on transportation
infrastructure at a regional scale, investigating risks and impacts on coastal ports, road, air,
rail, and public transit systems in the central Gulf Coast, with a study area stretching from
Houston/Galveston, Texas, to Mobile, Alabama. The study assessed likely changes in
temperature and precipitation patterns, sea-level rise, and increasing severity and
frequency of tropical storms. Phase 1 then explored how these changes could impact
transportation systems.

Gulf Coast Phase 2

Phase 2 focuses on the Mobile, Alabama, region -- with the goal of enhancing regional
decisionmakers' ability to understand potential impacts on specific critical components of
infrastructure and to evaluate adaptation options. In Mobile, the U.S. DOT is assessing the
vulnerability of the most critical transportation assets to climate change impacts. The U.S.
DOT will then develop risk management tools to help transportation system planners,
owners, and operators determine which systems and assets to protect and how to do so.
The methods and tools developed under Phase 2 are intended to be replicable to other
regions throughout the country. Phase 2 is scheduled to be completed in 2013.

Appendix B:
Climate Effects and Impacts

Table B1: Impacts of temperature on highway operations and infrastructure.
Source: FHWA (2010)

Climate Effects	Impacts on Infrastructure and Operations
Extreme Rutting. Source: www.asphaltwa.com **Increases in very hot days and heat waves (higher high temperatures, increased duration of heat waves)**	• Increased thermal expansion of bridge joints and paved surfaces, causing possible degradation. • Concerns regarding pavement integrity, traffic related rutting and migration of liquid asphalt, greater need for maintenance of roads and pavement. • Limits on periods of construction activity, and more night time work. • Vehicle overheating and tire degradation. • Maintenance and construction costs for roads and bridges are likely to increase as temperatures increase. • Stress on bridge integrity due to temperature expansion of concrete joints, steel, asphalt, protective cladding, coats and sealants. • Asphalt degradation, resulting in possible short term loss of public access or increased congestion of sections of road and highway during repair and replacement .
Decreases in very cold days	• Regional changes in snow and ice removal costs and environmental impacts from salt and chemical use. • Fewer cold-related restrictions for maintenance workers.
Later onset of seasonal freeze and earlier onset of seasonal thaw	• Changes in seasonal weight restrictions. • Changes in seasonal fuel requirements. • Improved mobility and safety associated with a reduction in winter weather. • Longer construction season in colder areas. • Freeze-thaw conditions increasing frost heaves and potholes restricting loads on roads.

Table B2: Impacts of precipitation on highway operations and infrastructure.
Source: FHWA(2010)

Climate Effects	Impacts on Infrastructure and Operations
 **NJ 287 collapse from Hurricane Irene.** *Source: NJ DOT* Increases in intense precipitation events	• Increases in weather-related delays and traffic disruptions. • Increased flooding of evacuation routes. • Increases in flooding of roadways and tunnels. • Increases in road washout, landslides and mudslides that damage roadways. • Drainage systems likely to be overloaded more frequently and severely, causing backups and street flooding. • Areas where flooding is already common will face more frequent and severe problems. • If soil moisture levels become too high, structural integrity of roads, bridges, and tunnels (especially where they are already under stress) could be compromised. • Standing water will have adverse effects on road base. • Increased peak streamflow could affect the sizing requirement for bridges and culverts.
 **Trestle fire in eastern Washington** *Source: Image from Washington State Department of Transportation, Climate Impacts Vulnerability Assessment, November 2011.* Increases in drought conditions	• Increased susceptibility to wildfires, causing road closures due to fire threat or reduced visibility. • Increased risk of mudslides in areas deforested by wildfires.

Slope Failure. SR 12. Source WSDOT

Changes in seasonal precipitation
and river flow patterns

- Benefits for safety and reduced interruptions if frozen precipitation shifts to rainfall.
- Increased risk of floods, landslides, slow failures and damage to roads if precipitation changes from snow to rain in winter and spring thaws.
- Increased variation in wet/dry spells and decrease in available moisture may cause road foundations to degrade.
- Degradation, failure and replacement of road structures due to increases in ground and foundation movement, shrinkage and changes in groundwater.
- Increased maintenance and replacement costs of road infrastructure.
- Short term loss of public access or increased congestion to sections of road and highway.

Table B3: Impacts of storm intensity on highway operations and infrastructure.
Source: FHWA(2010)

Climate Effects	Impacts on Infrastructure and Operations
Hurricane Damage from Wave Action to Highway 90 in Bay St Louis, MS Source: Illinoisphoto.com Increases in storm intensity (leading to higher storm surges, stronger winds, flooding)	- More frequent and potentially more extensive emergency evacuations. - More debris on roads, interrupting travel and shipping. - Bridges, signs, overhead cables and other tall structures are at risk from increased wind speeds. - Increased threat to stability of bridge decks. - Decreased expected life-time of highways exposed to storm surge. - Risk of immediate flooding, damage caused by force of water and secondary damage caused by collisions with debris. - Erosion of coastal highways and land supporting coastal infrastructure. - Damage to signs, lighting fixtures, and supports - Reduced drainage rate of low-lying land after rainfall and flooding events.

Table B4: Impacts of sea level rise on operations and highway infrastructure.
Source: FHWA(2010)

Climate Effects	Impacts on Infrastructure and Operations
 *Three breaches in NC12 after Hurricane Irene Photo Credit: Tom MacKenzie, US FWS* Rising sea levels (leading to higher storm surge, increased salinity of rivers and estuaries, flooding)	• Amplifies effect of storm surge, causing more frequent interruptions to coastal and low-lying roadway travel due to storm surges. • Amplifies effect of storm surge, causing more severe storm surges requiring evacuation. • Permanent inundation of roads or low lying feeder roads in coastal areas. Reduces route options/redundancy. • More frequent or severe flooding of underground tunnels and low-lying infrastructure. • As the sea level rises, the coastline will change and highways that were not previously at risk to storm surge and wave damage may be exposed in the future. • Erosion of road base and bridge supports. • Highway embankments at risk of subsidence/heave. • Bridge scour. • Reduced clearance under bridges. • Increased maintenance and replacement costs of tunnel infrastructure.

Glossary

Excerpted from *Impacts of Climate Variability and Change on Transportation Systems and Infrastructure—Gulf Coast Study*, US Department of Transportation, (2008) (GC1), and *Adapting to the Impacts of Climate Change*, America's Climate Choices: Panel on Adapting to the Impacts of Climate Change, National Research Council, (2010). (ACC)

Adaptation
Adjustment in natural or human systems to a new or changing environment that exploits beneficial opportunities or moderates negative effects. (ACC)

Adaptive Capacity
The ability of a system to adjust to climate change (including climate variability and extremes) to moderate potential damages, to take advantage of opportunities, or to cope with the consequences. (GC1)

Exposure
The combination of stress associated with climate-related change (sea level rise, changes in temperature, frequency of severe storms) and the probability, or likelihood, that this stress will affect transportation infrastructure. (GC1)

Extreme Weather Event
An event that is rare within its statistical reference distribution at a particular place. Definitions of "rare" vary, but an extreme weather event would normally be as rare as or rarer than the 10th or 90th percentile. By definition, the characteristics of what is called "extreme weather" may vary from place to place. Extreme weather events may typically include floods and droughts. (GC1)

Resilience
A capability to anticipate, prepare for, respond to, and recover from significant multi-hazard threats with minimum damage to social well-being, the economy, and the environment. (ACC)

Risk
A combination of the magnitude of potential consequence(s) of climate change impacts(s) and the likelihodd that the consequence(s) will occur. (ACC)

Vulnerability
The degree to which a system is susceptible to, or unable to cope with, adverse effects of climate change, including climate variability and extremes. Vulnerability is a function of the character, magnitude, and rate of climate variation to which a system is exposed, its sensitivity, and its adaptive capacity. (ACC)

References

California Department of Transportation, *Guidance on Incorporating Sea Level Rise*, 2011.

Eugene Mulero and Julia Pyper, "As states scramble to adapt, DOT pledges $13M in first of many likely cash infusions," *Greenwire*, October 21, 2012.

Federal Highway Administration, *Adaptation Peer Exchanges Final Report*, August 2012.

Federal Highway Administration, *Assessing Criticality in Transportation Planning*, 2011.

Federal Highway Administration, "Eligibility of Activities to Adapt To Climate Change and Extreme Weather Events under the Federal-Aid and Federal Lands Highway Program," 2012.

Federal Highway Administration, *Regional Climate Change Effects: Useful Information for Transportation Agencies*, 2010.

Federal Transit Administration, *Flooded Bus Barns and Buckled Rails: Public Transportation and Climate Change Adaptation*, 2011.

Metropolitan Transportation Commission, California Department of Transportation, Bay Conservation and Development Commission, *Adapting to Rising Tides: Transportation Vulnerability and Risk Assessment Pilot Project: Briefing Book*, November 2011.

National Academy of Sciences, *Adapting to the Impacts of Climate Change*, 2010

National Oceanic and Atmospheric Administration, Coastal Services Center. *Coastal Inundation Mapping Guidebook*. Charleston, South Carolina, 2009

National Oceanic and Atmospheric Administration, *Technical Considerations for Use of Geospatial Data in Sea Level Change Mapping and Assessment*, 2010.

New Jersey Transportation Planning Authority, *Climate Change Vulnerability and Risk Assessment of New Jersey's Transportation Infrastructure*, April 2012.

Oahu Metropolitan Planning Organization, *Transportation Asset Climate Change Risk Assessment*, November 2011.

Slater, Gregory I., "Climate Change Adaptation: Maryland State Highway Administration," Presentation to U.S. Department of Transportation, March 30, 2011.

Thomas et al., "Effects of Climate Change on the National Flood Insurance Program in the United States – Riverine Flooding." *Watershed Management 2010*, ASCE, 2011.

U.S. Climate Change Science Program, *Coastal Sensitivity to Sea-Level Rise: A Focus on the Mid-Atlantic Region*, 2009 http://www.climatescience.gov/Library/sap/sap4-1/final-report/

U.S. Department of Transportation, Policy Statement on Climate Change Adaptation, June 2011.

U.S. Department of Transportation, *Impacts of Climate Change and Variability on Transportation Systems and Infrastructure: Gulf Coast Study*, 2008.

U.S. Global Change Research Program, *Global Climate Change Impacts in the United States*, June 2009.

University of Virginia and Virginia Department of Transportation, *Assessing Vulnerability and Risk of Climate Change Effects on Transportation Infrastructure, Hampton Roads, VA Pilot,* November 2011.

Washington State Department of Transportation, *Climate Impacts Vulnerability Assessment*, November 2011.

Washington State Department of Transportation, *Guidance for Project-Level Greenhouse Gas and Climate Evaluations*, March 2012.

www.ingramcontent.com/pod-product-compliance
Lightning Source LLC
Chambersburg PA
CBHW080445290526
45791CB00008BA/2609